"North offers sound, useful information presented in a straight-forward, logical and readable manner. He stresses the recreational value of rivers in promoting river conservation. His approach is cautious and conservative, his writing sensible and sensitive.

While the book will no doubt increase recreational use of Washington rivers, it will also spread it out, for he introduces numerous 'lesser-known' rivers. The book is environmentally sound, with a strong conservation ethic running through it that would make Aldo Leopold proud."

—Verne Huser, Books Editor
RIVER RUNNER Magazine

"I've run many Washington rivers, but the value of this guide is in its descriptions of several that I didn't know existed, or had looked at but dismissed for lack of information—such as the Entiat, Lower Cispus and the Stehekin, plus a post-volcano report on the Toutle."

—Dave Harrison, Publisher
CANOE Magazine

"*Washington Whitewater* 2 gives you 17 good reasons, if you are an intermediate-to-advanced kayaker, to get out of your easy chair and onto the river . . . everything you need to know about Washington's better-kept whitewater secrets, from the Idaho border to the Olympics. A valuable sequel to *Washington Whitewater.*"

—Bob Mottram, Outdoor Writer
TACOMA NEWS-TRIBUNE

"Douglass North details rivers to run where few people know there are rivers. His work will help save Washington whitewater from the hands of the engineers. Buy the book, use it, and never curse the rain again, because it's what keeps the water white."

—Terry Richard, Sports Writer
PORTLAND OREGONIAN

"Whitewater enthusiasts will be impressed with North's research and the details he presents for each float. Best of all, the book looks out not only for boaters, but also for the rivers."

—Rich Landers, Outdoors Editor
SPOKESMAN-REVIEW

WASHINGTON
2
WHITEWATER

by
Douglass A. North

photography by
Lorrie H. North

The Mountaineers, Seattle

The Mountaineers: Organized 1906
" . . . to explore and study the mountains, forests,
and watercourses of the Northwest."

© 1987 by The Mountaineers

Published by The Mountaineers
306 2nd Avenue West, Seattle, Washington 98119

Published simultaneously in Canada by Douglas & McIntyre
1615 Venables Street, Vancouver, B. C. V5L 2H1

Manufactured in the United States of America

Edited by Paula Younkin
Designed by Bridget Culligan
Cover photos: Front—Surfing the Chiwawa. Back—Rafting the Kalama

Title photo: A taste of White Lightning, Upper Cispus.

Library of Congress Cataloging in Publication Data

North, Douglass A.
    Washington whitewater 2.

    Includes index.
    1. Rafting (Sports)--Washington (State)--Guide-
books.   2. White-water canoeing--Washington (State)--
Guide-books.   3. Washington (State)--Description and
travel--1981-   --Guide-books.   I. Title.   II. Title:
Washington whitewater two.   III. Title: Washington white
water 2.
GV776.W2N68   1987   917.97   87-1637
ISBN 0-89886-134-9

0 9 8 7
5 4 3 2 1

Contents

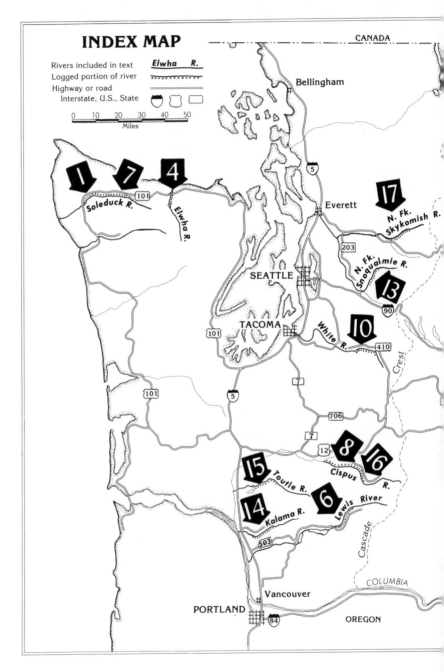

INDEX MAP

Rivers included in text   *Elwha   R.*
Logged portion of river   ∙∙∙∙∙∙∙∙∙∙∙∙∙∙
Highway or road
   Interstate, U.S., State

0   10   20   30   40   50
Miles

CANADA

Bellingham

Everett

SEATTLE

TACOMA

Soleduck R.

Elwha R.

N. Fk. Skykomish R.

N. Fk. Snoqualmie R.

White R.

Cispus R.

Toutle R.

Kalama R.

Lewis River

Crest

Cascade

COLUMBIA

Vancouver

PORTLAND

OREGON

1   7   4   17   13   10   8   16   15   6   14

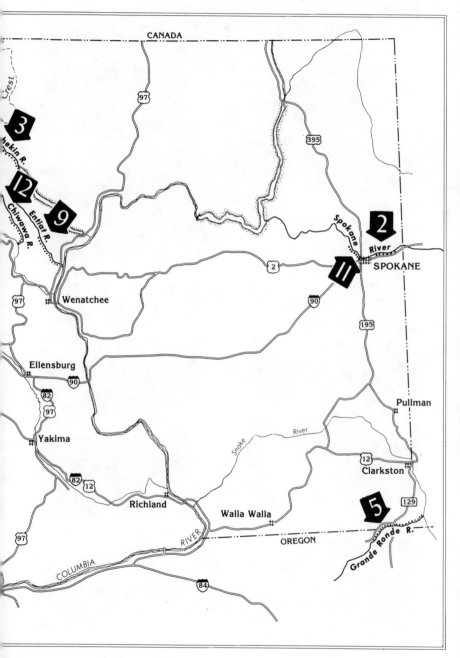

CANADA

3

Stehekin R.

12

9

Entiat R.

Chiwawa R.

Chelan R.

97

395

Spokane

2

River

SPOKANE

2

11

97

Wenatchee

90

195

Ellensburg

90

82

97

Pullman

Yakima

Snake

River

82

12

12

Clarkston

Richland

Walla Walla

5

129

97

OREGON

Grande Ronde R.

COLUMBIA

RIVER

84

Curly Creek Falls, Lewis River

Preface

River guidebooks take two basic approaches. One paints a general picture of the river, provides the essential information on put-ins, take-outs and river difficulty, and leaves the reader to explore the river himself. The other approach provides the reader with all of the verifiable information possible on the river, including descriptions and locations of rapids, landmarks and possible campsites. Each approach has advantages and disadvantages; some people may prefer one to the other.

The principal advantage of the less detailed guidebook is that it forces the boater to rely on his own resources. Its advocates point out that river channels constantly change, so recording the location of all rapids and landmarks as if they were static could be misleading.

The detailed river logs in this book obviously place it in the second category. These logs have several advantages:

1. They allow the boater who has never run the river to figure out where he is.

2. They allow boaters to choose put-ins and take-outs for the part of the river they wish to run.

3. They provide a graphical representation of the difficulty and intensity of each part of the trip.

4. They allow government agencies to precisely locate the important rapids and the most scenic sections for river conservation purposes.

5. They keep the author honest. Providing a detailed river log is impossible without having actually run the river, usually several times. Some authors are willing to include in their guidebooks rivers they have heard about, but have never run. Their "information" is often woefully inaccurate.

The first *Washington Whitewater*, published three years ago, has been well received. It gives boaters reliable information about a variety of Washington trips, some heavily, and some lightly, used.

An important reason for writing a guidebook is to promote river conservation. *Washington Whitewater* has introduced many boaters to the beauty and excitement of the rivers of this state. It has helped build a constituency of boaters to protect these rivers. A politically vigorous group of Washington boaters is vital to saving our free-flowing rivers. Over 200 dam license applications are pending for hydroelectric projects on Washington rivers. We organized too late to save the last two miles of the lower Cispus run, which is in this book. In a few years, the bottom 1.7 miles of the river will disappear beneath the slack waters behind the Cowlitz Falls project. A battle now rages to save the North Fork of the Snoqualmie from inundation by a water supply project. There have been dams proposed on many of the rivers in this book, including the Grande Ronde, Kalama, Cispus, Lewis and Chiwawa. To save these rivers, boaters must actively oppose these projects.

Washington Whitewater has also informed key government officials that the rivers are boated and should be protected and managed for recreation. The Forest Service, Federal Energy Regulatory Commission and the Northwest Power Planning Council frequently make decisions that affect the future of our rivers. If these agencies don't know that the rivers are boated, no consideration will be given to boating in their plans. Publishing boaters' guidebooks is the surest way to gain governmental recognition of the recreational value of our rivers.

Washington Whitewater 2 is designed to promote continued river conservation work. It will introduce you to many new rivers and, hopefully, get you involved in their protection. Concerned whitewater boaters in the Northwest have formed Friends of Whitewater, with chapters in Washington, Oregon, Idaho and Montana. We cover the same geographic region as the Northwest Power Planning Council. Friends of Whitewater has taken an active role in the Northwest Rivers Study conducted by the Power Planning Council to determine future dam sites in the Northwest. We have intervened as a party in Federal Energy Regulatory Commission dam licensing proceedings, participated in the planning process with the National Forests and, along with the Washington Wilderness Coalition, begun work on a Wild & Scenic Rivers bill for Washington.

If you enjoy Washington's rivers, get involved!

Friends of Whitewater
P. O. Box 88
Seattle, WA 98111–088

Acknowledgments

I would like to express my thanks to the River Rats who helped run and log the rivers in this book: Bob Johnson, Gary Korb, Mark Lowe, Lorrie North, Mike and Cindy Smith, Doug and Sharon Swan and Carol Volk.

I also gratefully acknowledge the assistance and kind permission of John Garren to use the river log system that he developed in *Oregon River Tours* and *Idaho River Tours*. He developed much of the river data in the introduction to explain the background and use of the river log system.

Finally, thanks go to Professor Joel M. Andress and geography students Robert Adams, Cheryl Beedle and Hank Riddle at Central Washington University who drew the maps for this book.

Crashing Smoothrock Falls, *Upper Cispus River*

Introduction

This guidebook is for intermediate, advanced and expert rafters or kayakers who already know the basics of controlling their boats in rapids. It is *not* for beginners to use by themselves. If you do not already know how to handle a raft or kayak in class 2 water, you are not yet ready to undertake the trips in this book without expert help. The beginning boater should look first to books on technique and equipment, such as the *Whitewater River Book* by Ron Watters.

Because it is essential to know the water level of a river in order to run it safely, I selected rivers for which representative gauge readings are available. To increase the likelihood of a pleasant experience for everyone, I chose rivers that normally have sufficient water to allow you to run them in a raft for at least three weeks from April through September.

Although some smaller rivers have enough water to be boated nearly every year, their frequent log jams make boating difficult. I have excluded rivers with insufficient flow to move the logs to one side of the river. This does not mean that you will never encounter a log all the way across these rivers, but it is unusual. However, you should always remain alert.

The original *Washington Whitewater* and this book describe nearly all the rivers in this state which (1) have significant whitewater, (2) allow rafting, as well as kayaking during the warm months of the year, (3) have fairly reliable water level information available on them, and (4) do not suffer from chronic log jams.

River Classification

There are formal, recognized methods of classifying rivers according to difficulty. This is of particular advantage to the beginning boater so that he may select rivers, or sections of rivers, within his capability. The following is a summary of the International River Classification System:

Class 1. Easy and Novice

Sand banks, bends without difficulty, occasional small rapids with waves regular and low. Correct course easy to find. River velocity less than hard backpaddling speed from 0–4 miles per

Eagle Cliff Drop *will disappear if another dam is built on the Lewis River.*

hour. Spray cover or decking for canoes unnecessary. River drop approximately 0–5 feet per mile.

Class 2. Medium or Intermediate

Fairly frequent but unobstructed rapids, regular waves, easy eddies and river bends. Course easy to recognize. River velocity occasionally exceeding hard backpaddling, velocity from 2–6 miles per hour. Spray covers for canoe useful. River drop 5–15 feet per mile.

Class 3. Difficult or Expert

Maneuvering in rapids necessary. Powerful eddies, standing waves, course difficult to read, scouting required, lining should be considered. Canoes require spray covers. River drop 10–25 feet per mile. River velocity 4–8 miles per hour.

Class 4. Very Difficult or Expert

Difficult broken water, long extended rapids, standing waves and eddies, powerful hydraulics, course difficulty requires scouting, lining may be necessary. River drop exceeds 30 feet per mile. River velocities over 6 miles per hour.

Class 5. Exceedingly Difficult

River conditions are seldom attempted even by the very experienced.

Class 6. Dangerous

River running involves substantial hazard to life.

It is almost impossible to rate a whole river under this system, but the classification is useful in describing a particular rapid. Generally, any major rapid is class 3 or more and should be approached with some caution. Ratings in this book are conservative. Thus, if there is a question between two rating classes, the higher rating is used.

You should keep in mind that each rapid differs slightly at every water level. However, the same rapids present the most serious challenges on a given stretch regardless of the water level. Ultimately, it is your responsibility to match your ability to the river you intend to run.

In order to provide some help to you in evaluating the difficulty of the rivers in this book, the trips are described from *least* to *most* difficult—from the Lower Soleduck to the North Fork of the Skykomish. The runs are grouped into three sections: intermediate, advanced and expert. An intermediate boater knows the rules of whitewater safety, understands hypothermia and basic river hydraulics, and can control his boat in moderate rapids—class 2 with some easy class 3. The intermediate runs either have rapids no more difficult than class 2 or the major rapids can be easily inspected from the road before putting in, allowing you to decide whether you are capable of running them before you start.

An advanced boater thoroughly understands river hydraulics, runs class 3 rapids with confidence and has good river reading skills. All of the advanced runs have either demanding class 3 rapids that cannot be easily seen from the road or they have nearly continuous class 2 and 3 rapids that require substantial experience to run safely.

An expert boater has excellent river reading skills, runs class 3 rapids without scouting and remains confident in class 4 water. The expert runs involve class 4 rapids and, often, nearly continuous class 3.

Boaters in open canoes should approach these rivers with great caution. The intermediate rivers can be canoed by very good canoeists, after careful scouting. All the advanced rivers have class 3 rapids which will swamp an open canoe. Only expert whitewater canoeists running the river at low water are likely to make it down these rivers with both themselves and their canoe in one piece. The expert rivers verge on being impossible to canoe even for expert whitewater canoeists.

Decked canoes are capable of running any water that a kayak can, and all references to kayaks in this book include decked canoes as well.

Washington Rivers

Boaters from other states who are not familiar with continuous rapids should approach Washington rivers with caution. In many other parts of the country, the rivers are pool and drop with substantial stretches of calm water between the rapids. Very few Washington rivers are pool and drop. Most have continuous fast water that offers little opportunity to recover from an upset before the next rapid. Some of the rivers have such continuous rapids that eddies are rare enough to be landmarks.

Washington rivers have continuous fast water because their river valleys are fairly broad and smoothly sloped. The valleys were formed by glaciers in the last ice age and have the U shape characteristic of glacial valleys. Washington had particularly heavy glaciers in the last ice age due to its northern location and its heavy precipitation.

Because the glaciers carved broad valleys with even gradients, Washington's highway engineers have built roads along nearly all of the major river valleys in the state. (Due to dense vegetation, however, the roads are not usually visible from the rivers.) This is in contrast with other states (such as California, Oregon and Idaho) that have large river valleys with no roads in them. Often the river valleys in these states are narrow defiles cut solely by the river's erosion. Thus, highway engineers have frequently avoided the river valleys in favor of the plateaus between.

Selecting a River

Know your abilities and select a river suitable for your skill level. Generally at least one intermediate, advanced or expert run is at a runnable water level at all times from April through July. The Runnable Seasons table (page 17) will help you pick a river that is likely to be at a good water level.

Water Level

Water level is one of the most important factors a boater should consider. There is a relatively narrow range of water levels for any river that makes for a good trip. Below some minimum level, the stream velocity decreases, the rocks (stream roughness) become more troublesome and the trip more difficult. Conversely, above a certain level, the stream velocity becomes so high and the river hydraulics so powerful as to make safe boating impossible. This is particularly true on rivers with very high average slopes like many of those in this book.

Fortunately, government agencies maintain a large system of stream gauges on almost all major rivers. The gauge heights are translated into cubic feet per second, abbreviated as cfs, a measure of the volume of water passing by the gauge in one second. Each whitewater trip in this book is referenced to a specific water level on the particular trip, along with recommended water levels. I have tried to use representative gauges wherever possible. Sometimes it has been necessary, however, to use a gauge on another part of the river or another river, because it is the only one from which up-to-date readings can be obtained.

Kayakers can generally run a river at a lower water level than rafters; thus, many of the descriptions mention a lower minimum water level suitable for kayakers. The general recommended level indicated is the one for rafts because kayakers will also generally find the higher water level more enjoyable, with better holes to play in.

You can check on the current water level by calling the tape-recorded message prepared by the National Oceanic and Atmospheric Administration (NOAA) at (206) 526-8530. The tape is updated every Monday, Wednesday and Friday morning from April through November. From December through March the tape provides Steelheader's Hotline information on river levels. If you can't get the information you need from the tape, call NOAA at (206) 526-6087. For some rivers I've listed another agency that can provide gauge information as well. The tape should be your main source of information because the other agencies are primarily concerned with flood control and warnings and do not welcome calls from river runners. Call them only if you cannot get the information you need from the tape.

The Runnable Seasons table shows you the time of year when the average flow of the river is within the recommended water level. Of course, the river frequently varies from the average flow, so check the water level. Since most people like to boat in the warm months of the year, the times listed as best at the beginning of each chapter are only the warmer months.

RUNNABLE SEASONS

	Trip	Recommended Water Level (in cubic feet per second) and gauge location.	J	F	M	A	M	J	J	A	S	O	N	D
1	Lower Soleduck	1,200–3,000 McDonald Bridge	▬	▬	▬	▬							▬	▬
2	Upper Spokane	4,000–19,000 Spokane	▬	▬	▬	▬							▬	
3	Stehekin	1,500–5,000 Stehekin				▬	▬	▬	▬					
4	Elwha	1,200–2,600 McDonald Bridge	▬	▬	▬	▬	▬	▬					▬	▬
5	Grande Ronde	1,500–9,000 Troy	▬	▬	▬	▬	▬	▬						
6	Lewis	1,200–2,800 Randle	▬	▬	▬	▬							▬	▬
7	Upper Soleduck	1,200–3,000 McDonald Bridge	▬	▬	▬	▬	▬						▬	▬
8	Lower Cispus	1,400–3,500 Randle	▬			▬	▬	▬						▬
9	Entiat	5,500–11,000 Peshastin					▬	▬						
10	White	1,000–3,400 Buckley	▬	▬	▬	▬	▬	▬	▬	▬			▬	
11	Lower Spokane	4,000–19,000 Spokane	▬	▬	▬	▬							▬	
12	Chiwawa	5,000–10,000 Peshastin					▬	▬						
13	Snoqualmie, North Fork	600–1,600 North Fork	▬			▬	▬						▬	
14	Kalama	1,100–3,200 Kalama	▬	▬	▬	▬						▬		
15	Toutle	800–2,500 Kalama			▬	▬	▬					▬		
16	Upper Cispus	1,500–2,600 Randle				▬	▬						▬	▬
17	Skykomish, North Fork	6,000–12,000 Goldbar				▬	▬							

Slope

River slope is usually measured by boaters in feet of river drop per mile. It can be scaled from conventional U. S. Geological Survey contour maps. Steep slopes have high river velocity and will usually, but not necessarily, have difficult rapids. The slope listed at the beginning of each chapter is the average for the trip.

Most of the trips in this book have high average slopes. Many famous whitewater trips in other states have more gentle slopes. The Colorado in the Grand Canyon has a slope of 8 feet per mile, the Salmon River in Idaho 12 feet per mile. In this book, the Lower Spokane and the Lower Soleduck have slopes in this range, but most of the trips have much higher slopes, ranging up to the North Fork of the Skykomish at 56 feet per mile. High slopes make for faster trips and more constant whitewater.

Roughness

River roughness greatly influences river difficulty. The rocky, "rough" stream channel provides the basis for a wide variety of stream hydraulics that forms rapids.

A relatively uniform stream slope and smooth channel (such as the lower Stehekin) usually provide easy river boating. Rough channels with steeper river slopes often end up with names like *Hollywood Gorge Falls*, *White Lightning* and *The Minefield*.

Difficulty

The factors of water level, slope and roughness are the major criteria to consider in evaluating river difficulty. All of these factors play a role in the formation of rapids, and rapids are the principal determinant for river difficulty. Several other factors are more subjective, such as ease of rescue, water temperature, or remoteness of the river. Indirectly, all of these factors are considered when evaluating the rapid's classifications.

Once you have found a river of suitable difficulty and water level, look at that chapter and see whether the scenery, camping, and rapids descriptions suit your needs. If you seek solitude, consult the table of "Relative Use."

Length of Runs

Some of the runs are much longer than others and lend themselves to overnight trips if you would like to do some river camp-

RELATIVE USE

	River	Commercial Use	General Use
1	Lower Soleduck	Light	Moderate*
2	Upper Spokane	Light	Heavy
3	Stehekin	Light	Light
4	Elwha	Light	Moderate
5	Grande Ronde	Moderate	Moderate
6	Lewis	None	Light
7	Upper Soleduck	Light	Light*
8	Lower Cispus	Moderate	Moderate
9	Entiat	None	Light
10	White	Light	Light
11	Lower Spokane	Light	Moderate
12	Chiwawa	Light	Light
13	Snoqualmie, North Fork	None	Moderate
14	Kalama	None	Light
15	Toutle	Light	Light
16	Upper Cispus	None	Light
17	Skykomish, North Fork	Light	Light

*Soleduck use is light before and after fishing season and moderate during fishing season when many fishermen are on the river in drift boats.

ing. The Grande Ronde and Upper Soleduck would make good overnight trips, as would both the Upper and Lower Cispus, run as one trip. The following table lists the length of each trip.

WHITEWATER RUNS*

Rating		River	Length of Run in miles
Intermediate Rivers	**1**	Lower Soleduck	7
	2	Upper Spokane	6
	3	Stehekin	10
	4	Elwha	6
Advanced Rivers	**5**	Grande Ronde	45
	6	Lewis	6
	7	Upper Soleduck	24
	8	Lower Cispus	17
	9	Entiat	14
	10	White	14
	11	Lower Spokane	6
	12	Chiwawa	15
	13	Snoqualmie, North Fork	6
	14	Kalama	10
Expert Rivers	**15**	Toutle	10
	16	Upper Cispus	9
	17	Skykomish, North Fork	11

*This ranking is based on the difficulty of controlling your boat. Estimating the danger to swimmers in the event of upset would be different. As an example, the White's log jams present a great danger of death to swimmers who may be swept into them. Thus, it requires less skill to boat the White than the Lower Spokane, but there is greater danger in boating the White.

Can you handle Class 4 water? Know your abilities.

Using the River Map and Log

The river map and log contain most of the information you need on the river. Both the log and map use the standard river convention of placing upstream at the bottom of the page and downstream at the top so that the log and map show the river flowing away from you. The maps and logs correlate so that you can see where you are on both simultaneously by referring to river miles. River miles are counted from the mouth so that they go down in number as you go down the river.

The river log depicts features that can actually be seen by a boater on the river. Thus, some of the maps show features that are useful reference points but do not appear on the logs and some of the text refers to features that are not on the logs because these features can't be seen from the river. The maps often show a larger area than indicated on the logs so that the user can get oriented more easily for making shuttles.

The log and map can be taped on the cowling of a kayak or the frame of a raft. Only a few symbols are necessary to describe most of the things a boater can identify on the river. Of course, it isn't possible to follow the log while running a river with continuous difficult rapids such as the North Fork of the Skykomish or the Upper Cispus. On these rivers, you consult the log whenever you stop, and check on the landmarks which you need to remember for the next portion of the trip.

Remember that the river logs are not engraved in stone. River channels can change overnight with a flood, landslide, earthquake or even a big tree falling across the river. If you see anything peculiar, such as freshly toppled trees that still have green leaves on them piling up around a bend, get out and scout from shore!

The river logs are measured in units of time rather than distance. This is because the speed with which a boater progresses downriver changes frequently as the slope of the riverbed changes. Time remains constant, however, and you can easily gain a sense of how long it will take to get to the next rapid in comparison with how long it took you to get to the last one. I don't

Symbols for the Logs

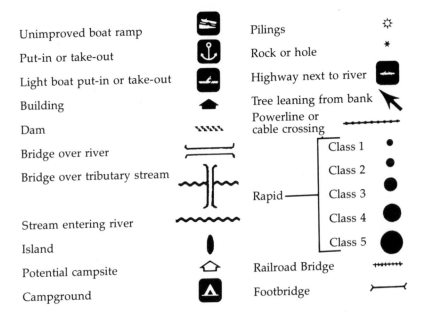

Unimproved boat ramp		Pilings	
Put-in or take-out		Rock or hole	
Light boat put-in or take-out		Highway next to river	
Building		Tree leaning from bank	
Dam		Powerline or cable crossing	
Bridge over river		Rapid — Class 1	
Bridge over tributary stream		Class 2	
		Class 3	
		Class 4	
Stream entering river		Class 5	
Island			
Potential campsite		Railroad Bridge	
Campground		Footbridge	

expect that you will actually use a watch to time your progress downriver, but only that the log will give you a feel for how long it will take you to get to the next point of interest.

In planning your trip, you should expect that the total time on the river, including stops, will be about 1½ to 2 times the amount of time shown on the log.

Relative Drift Time

The relative drift time for various boats differs significantly. Log times in this book are for a 10-man raft at a particular river stage. (If you wonder why a raft was always used, try keeping track of time while taking detailed notes and paddling a kayak.) For the same type boat and approximate river stage there is little difference in time. Kayaks, however, move downriver about one and one-half times faster than a raft (unless they are playing in a hole, of course); consequently, kayakers should find that it takes them only about two-thirds the time shown in the log to cover any portion of the run.

Safety

Anyone using this book on a river should already be very familiar with whitewater safety. Just as a reminder, however, the following points should be borne in mind:

1. **Wear a lifejacket at all times.** The biggest cause of death on a river, bar none, is the failure to wear a lifejacket. Everyone should wear a Coast Guard approved type I, III, or V lifejacket.

2. **Never boat a river beyond your ability.** You should always be capable of running the hardest rapid on the stretch of river that you intend to run. Know the River Classification System and your ability.

3. **Never boat a river at too high a water level.** This is probably the next biggest killer after failure to wear a lifejacket. Consequently, this book recommends a range of water levels for each river and tells you where to call to find out the gauge readings.

4. **Always be aware of the threat of hypothermia.** It is nearly always necessary to wear a wetsuit when running the rivers of western Washington. Most of the water in these rivers is recently melted ice and snow. Hypothermia strikes in three to five

Many Washington rivers have nearly continuous whitewater.

minutes. Wetsuits are often necessary in eastern Washington too, and wool clothing should always be kept handy.

5. Always boat with an organized group. There should be at least two boats in your party if both are large rafts (larger than six-man) and at least three boats if any are not large rafts. Everyone in the group should be trained in how to rescue boaters in the event of upset.

6. Be aware of the danger presented by sweepers and strainers. Sweepers and strainers are downed logs and brush in the river. They present a much greater danger of death to swimmers than do rocks because the water flowing through them can easily pin a swimmer under water. Boaters must be careful to stay away from brush and log jams.

7. Be aware of the danger presented by dams and weirs. These man-made river obstructions create perfect hydraulics which can prove deadly with only a 2 foot drop. They are the second most dangerous obstacles on a river after sweepers and strainers.

8. Wear a helmet at all times when you kayak and in class 4 or 5 water when you raft. The rocky channels generally present in class

4 or 5 rapids pose a considerable danger to the head of anyone thrown out of a boat. Kayakers should wear helmets at all times because of the ease with which they may suddenly find themselves upside-down.

Because of the difficulty of these runs, kayakers should be familiar with the Eskimo Roll, and all boaters should be prepared to remove a boat pinned on rocks.

Whitewater rafting and kayaking entails unavoidable risks that every river runner assumes, realizes and respects. This guide assumes that you understand those risks. The fact that a section of river is described in this book and is rated for difficulty does not mean that it necessarily will be safe for you. Rivers vary

Some rivers have unique scenery, such as these rock formations on the Lower Spokane.

greatly in difficulty and in the amount and kind of preparation needed to enjoy them safely. And because rivers are dynamic systems, conditions frequently change with the weather, seasons and other factors.

You minimize the risks by being knowledgeable, prepared, and alert. There is not space in this book for a general treatise on whitewater rafting or kayaking, but a number of good books and courses teach these skills. It is essential that you be aware both of your own limitations and of existing conditions at the time and place of your outing. If river conditions require greater skill or experience than you possess, or if factors such as weather or the condition of your craft, yourself, or your companions are such as to dangerously increase the risk of running a river, change your plans. It is better to have wasted a day or two than to invite serious injury or fatality.

These warnings are not intended to warn qualified whitewater boaters off the rivers described in this guide. Many people enjoy safe kayaking or rafting trips down these rivers every year. However, one element of the beauty, freedom, and excitement of river running is the presence of risks that do not confront us at home. When you kayak or raft down a whitewater river, you take on those risks. You can meet them safely, but only if you exercise your own independent judgment and common sense.

River Ethics

Part of river conservation is making sure that your enjoyment does not degrade the river's natural qualities or harm its fish and wildlife. If our children and grandchildren are to enjoy our rivers and the wild creatures that visit them, we must take care to leave the river environment no worse than we find it. To ensure the enjoyment of our rivers for everyone, keep the following rules in mind.

1. **Respect private property.** Don't put in, take out or stop on private property without the owner's permission. Certainly, don't take anything, such as fruit or wood. Nothing will restrict our use of rivers faster than alienating local landowners.

2. **Don't leave anything behind.** This applies to litter, equipment and even evidence of fire. Pack it *all* out.

3. **Use a stove or firepan.** Use of fire is not common on Washington

rivers because nearly all rivers can be run in one day, but if you have a fire, put it in a firepan. A firepan prevents charring the ground and killing the micro-organisms in the soil. It also makes packing the ashes out with you easy; and no one can tell that you had a fire. Always have a shovel along (in addition to your bailing bucket) anytime you have fire.

4. Dispose of human waste and waste water above the high water mark. It will decompose faster if buried in the top 6–8 inches of soil. Pack out all toilet paper in a plastic sack. Use biodegradable soap.

5. Respect the privacy of others. Don't stop to eat or camp where others have stopped; find your own site on downriver. Keep quiet while passing other groups on the river; they may be appreciating nature's tranquility.

6. Don't disturb wildlife. Many animals and birds nest and feed along rivers and can be seriously disturbed by boaters coming unnecessarily close, perhaps to take a picture.

River shorelines are a particularly fragile and much used environment. Treat them with respect so that we can continue to enjoy them in the future.

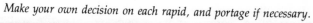

Make your own decision on each rapid, and portage if necessary.

1

Lower Soleduck

Logged at -	2,000 cfs McDonald Bridge gauge (early May)
Recommended water level -	1,200 to 3,000 cfs (varies)
Best time -	April to mid-June
Rating -	Intermediate
Water level information -	NOAA Tape (206) 526-8530 NOAA Information (206) 526-6087
River mile -	29.9 to 23.1; 6.8 miles
Time -	2 hours, 2 minutes; 3.4 mph
Elevation -	330' to 260'; 10' per mile

Salmon Hatchery to Salmon Drive

The Soleduck is named after the Sol Duc Hotsprings near its headwaters in Olympic National Park. The Indian spelling, Sol Duc, means "sparkling water." Indians believed that the water had magical, medicinal powers. Whatever the healing powers of the hotsprings may be, a trip on the river can be healing to the soul. The clear water, overhung by lush trees festooned with moss, teems with salmon and steelhead and flows through largely untouched banks. The Soleduck has magic.

Getting There
The Soleduck is paralleled by US 101 from a few miles north of Forks nearly to Lake Crescent, some 34 miles west of Port Angeles.

Put-ins and Take-outs
The put-in is the boat ramp at Soleduck River Salmon Hatchery near Sappho, some 12 miles north of Forks. From either direction the turn-off is about 0.2 mile after crossing a bridge over the Soleduck. Turn south on the dirt road, and take an immediate

The Lower Soleduck can be canoed if your canoe has
flotation and you are an experienced whitewater paddler.

right in the direction pointed by the small, white "Hatchery" sign. Take the gravel road parallel to the river downstream about 1.5 miles to the hatchery. The boat ramp is to your right.

The take-out is at another boat ramp just off Salmon Drive. Take the turn-off marked Salmon Drive from 101. The turn-off is about 6 miles north of Forks or about 6.5 miles from the turn-off to the salmon hatchery. Salmon Drive cuts along the side of the hill down to a bench of land by the river and there turns directly away from 101. Follow it toward the river for a couple of hundred yards, and take a right at the stop sign. Drive parallel to the river for another 0.3 mile and you will reach the Department of Game boat ramp.

Water Level

No gauge has up-to-date reports on the Soleduck, so the water level must be judged by the McDonald Bridge gauge on the Elwha,

The Soleduck is lined by lush vegetation.

the next basin over. The Elwha gauge provides a fairly good indication of conditions on the Soleduck, but certainly not an exact measurement. The Elwha gets more snow run-off than the Soleduck, so a higher reading is needed on the McDonald Bridge gauge later in the season than early on. What you are looking for is a somewhat greater than average flow in the spring. It is usually present after a good rain or after a couple days of hot weather that melts the snow. Recommended minimum and maximum levels for the Soleduck in spring are as follows:

	April	May 1–15	May 16–31	June 1–15	June 16–on
minimum	1,200	1,500	1,800	2,100	2,400
maximum	2,400	3,000	3,600	3,700	3,900

You have to use some good sense in making use of this table. It is based on average weather conditions. For example, in early May, if it has been colder and wetter than normal, look at the April figures. If it has been hotter and drier than normal, however, look at the late May figures. Also note that these are the recommended boating levels; you can scrape down the river with a lot less. Fishermen regularly take their drift boats down the Soleduck at least through mid-June every year, but they're looking for good fishing, not good boating.

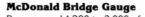

McDonald Bridge Gauge
Recommend 1,200 to 3,000 cfs

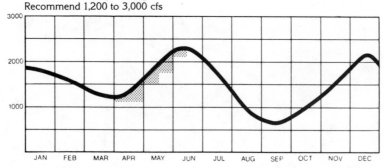

Most of the Soleduck rapids are boulder gardens.

Special Hazards

Fishermen are not really a special hazard, but remember that they were here first. Stay out of the way of their lines, particularly

The channel with the most water is often close to the bank.

if they have a fish on. Fishing season usually lasts from winter through March and begins again in late May, continuing through July. April and early May are good times to boat the Soleduck without getting in the way of the fishermen.

Scenery
The Soleduck is a very beautiful river with lots of wildlife living in its stream and along its banks. Except for scattered cabins, the thick foliage screens away the sights and sounds of civilization. I've seen deer, ducks, salmon and bald eagles while threading through bouldery drops and drifting on crystal clear pools.

Camping
Campsites provided by ITT Rayonier are available in the Tumbling Rapids Recreation Area right across US 101 from the turn-off to the salmon hatchery. Tumbling Rapids is usually open only from Memorial Day weekend through Labor Day, however. The State Department of Natural Resources (DNR) Wahlgren Memorial Campground, about three miles east of the turn-off to the salmon hatchery, toward Port Angeles on US 101, is open throughout the year.

Rapids
The mild rapids on this trip could be negotiated by good whitewater canoeists. They mostly consist of rock gardens, requiring considerable threading through boulders, but they do not have powerful hydraulics. **Tyee Rapids** provides some waves that can swamp a canoe, however.

Below the logged run, the river is almost entirely class 1, except for three class 2 rapids in the lower 23 miles of the river: Shuwah Rapids, at the mouth of Shuwah Creek, about a mile below Salmon Drive; Double Rapids, a few miles farther down, just below the US 101 bridge near Forks; and a rapid just above the mouth of the river. This lower section also has pleasant scenery, but homes and cabins along the banks are much more common and nearly all the land is privately owned.

SOLEDUCK RIVER

SALMON HATCHERY TO SALMON DRIVE

LEGEND

Road	
Bridge	
River mile	(26)
Boat Access	⚓
Campground	⛺
Rapid/class	Moss Garden / 3

Forks
6 miles

Iverson

Salmon Drive

(23)

(24)

101

Lake

(25)

Tyee Rapids / 2

(26)

Creek

(27)

N

(28)

Lake Pleasant

Bockman Creek

(29)

(30)

Fish Hatchery ⚓

101

(31)

Tumbling Rapids
Campground ⛺

Sappho

1   ½   0   1
miles

RIVER MILE	RIVER TIME	LEFT BANK	RAPIDS	RIGHT BANK	DESCRIPTION
					—Salmon Drive boat ramp
	2:00				
	55				
	50				—Lake Creek right
	45				
	40				
	35				
	30		●2		
RM 25	25		●2		—Run right
	20		●2		
	15				
	10		●2		—Tyee Rapids
	5		●2		
	1:00				
	55		●2		
	50				
	45				
	40				
	35				
	30				
	25				—Bockman Creek left
	20		●2		
	15		●2		
	10			TT	—Picnic shelter right
RM 30	5				—Run either side of island —Salmon Hatchery outlet left
	12:00				—Boat ramp —Dam and pump tower left

2

Upper Spokane

Logged at - 13,000 cfs Spokane gauge
Recommended water level - 4,000 to 19,000 cfs
Best time - April through June
Rating - Intermediate
Water level information - NOAA Tape (206) 526-8530
NOAA Information (206) 526-6087
Washington Water Power (509) 489-0500 (Ext. 2141)
River mile - 92.7 to 86.3; 6.4 miles
Time - 1 hour, 10 minutes; 5.5 mph
Elevation - 2,000' to 1,905'; 15' per mile

Harvard Park to "Walk-in-the-Wild" Park

The Upper Spokane provides good playspots and is also the classic training run for Spokane boaters. The name Spokane comes from a chief of the local Indian tribe who identified himself to early fur traders as Illim-Spokane or "chief of the sun people." You'll usually find sun when running the Spokane in May or June when the water levels are good. The trip is just class 2, but at lower water levels, a lateral wave in Sullivan Rapids can cause trouble for open canoes.

Getting There
The Upper Spokane parallels I-90 east of Spokane.

Put-ins and Take-outs
The put-in is reached by taking exit 296, labelled Liberty Lake, Otis Orchards, from I-90. Go north toward Otis Orchards 0.2 mile to the bridge over the river. Harvard Park is just downstream from the bridge on the right bank.

The take-out at Walk-in-the-Wild Park is reached by taking exit

289, labelled Pines Road, Opportunity, from I-90. Go north on Pines Road 0.8 mile, and turn right on the tree-lined road to Walk-in-the-Wild Park. Bear right when you come to the Y 0.7 mile down the road and right again onto a gravel road at a Y 0.1 mile farther. Turn left after another 0.1 mile, going through a narrow concrete overpass to the river.

An alternative put-in or take-out can be made on the right bank upstream from Sullivan Bridge by taking exit 291 from I-90 onto Sullivan Road.

You can lengthen the trip by 1.5 miles of class 1 water down to Plante Ferry State Park. The take-out there is on the right bank of the river, reached from Spokane by taking Upriver Drive.

Water Level

The Upper Spokane provides a good run at levels between 4,000 and 19,000 cfs. Above 19,000, the drops begin to wash out and there are very few playspots. In late June the gates on the dam at

Sullivan Rapids *has some good playspots.*

Post Falls, Idaho are gradually closed and the river drops rapidly. The sun is strong enough to warm the water significantly by mid-June, making it quite pleasant.

Spokane Gauge
Recommend 4,000 to 19,000 cfs

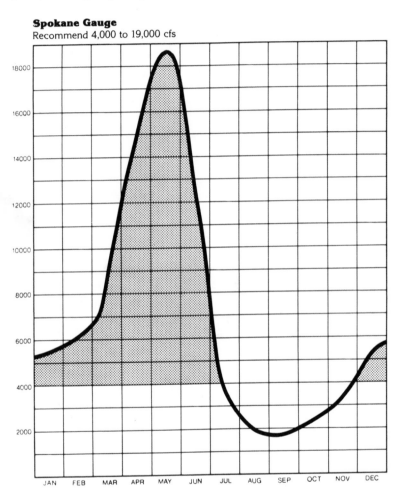

Special Hazards

Watch out for the Heli-jet jetboat which can go up- or down-river very fast. There are no significant rapids on this section of the river, yet people are killed on it nearly every year when they go tubing without lifejackets. It's a big river; treat it with respect.

The Upper Spokane is very popular with novice rafters.

Scenery
Although the run is very near Spokane, much of it is fairly pretty with scattered pine forests and a boulder-strewn river bed, particularly in the section from river log time 40 minutes to 1 hour.

Camping
Camping facilities are available at Riverside State Park, along the Spokane, downstream from the city. See the chapter on the Lower Spokane for directions to the Park.

Rapids
The rapids on this stretch are no more than class 2, though Sullivan Rapids can cause problems for inexperienced boaters. You can scout on the right bank.

Pines Road

Inland Empire
Zoo

(90)

(85.5)

(86)

(87)

SPOKANE RIVER

HARVARD PARK TO
"WALK IN THE WILD" PARK

Sullivan
Park

Sullivan Road

(88)

Sullivan Rapids / 2

(89)

LEGEND

Road	
Bridge	
River mile	(24)
Boat Access	
Campground	(A)
Rapid/class	El Nino / 4

(90)

Barker Rd.

(90)

(91)

N

1	½	0		1

Miles

(92)

Harvard
Park

Harvard Rd.

(93)

RIVER MILE	RIVER TIME	LEFT BANK	RAPIDS	RIGHT BANK	DESCRIPTION
	2:00				
	55				
	50				
	45				
	40				
	35				
	30				
	25				
	20				
	15				
	10	⚓		■	—Zoo left, pumping station for Kaiser plant right
	5				
	1:00		╪╪╪╪╪╪		—Powerlines followed by railroad bridge
	55				—Sullivan Bridge and Park
	50			⚓	
	45	♠	●2		—Fun waves
			●2		
	40		●2		—**Sullivan Rapids,** good playspot
		♠	•—•—•		—Powerlines, begin pine forested banks
	35	♠	●2		—Good kayak playspot, best at low water
RM 90	30		●2	■	—Mill right
			♠♠		
	25	♠	♠♠		—Barker Bridge
	20		♠♠♠		
	15		•—•—• ♠		
	10				
	5				
	12:00			⚓	—Harvard Bridge and Park

Lake Chelan can be breathtakingly still in early morning.

3

Stehekin

Logged at - 2,500 cfs Stehekin gauge
Recommended water level - 1,500 to 5,000 cfs
Best time - May to August
Rating - Intermediate
Water level information - NOAA Tape (206) 526-8530
NOAA Information (206) 526-6087
Chelan County Public Utility District
(PUD) (509) 663-8121
River mile - 10.1 to 0; 10.1 miles
Time - 1 hour, 50 minutes; 5.5 mph
Elevation - 1,525' to 1,100'; 42' per mile

Agnes Creek to Lake Chelan

The Stehekin is one of the most remote boatable rivers in Washington. Only the first 0.5 mile of the logged run involves serious whitewater (and that part can be easily avoided by putting in downstream a bit) but the scenery and campsites are gorgeous. Stehekin means "the way through" and the valley was a travel route through the mountains for the Indians.

Miners came to the Stehekin in the 1880s to work claims that went by such names as: Black Warrior, King Solomon and Emerald Park. The valley was homesteaded in the 1890s and soon became a mecca for tourists and hikers. The valley is now part of the Lake Chelan National Recreation Area, attached to North Cas-

There are many great hikes into the mountains out of Stehekin.

The Lady of the Lake *tied up at Stehekin Landing*

cades National Park and administered by the National Park Service.

Getting There

Getting there, as they say, is half the fun. In the case of the Stehekin, it's an adventure: you can't drive. There's no road to the Stehekin. Access is via the *Lady of the Lake,* a large passenger boat operated by the Lake Chelan Boat Company, Box W, Chelan, WA 98816, (509) 682-4584. From May 15 to October 15 the boat runs up and down the lake once a day, but call before you go, to check. (Off season the boat runs only Monday, Wednesday, Friday and Sunday.)

Unfortunately, the *Lady of the Lake* will not take kayaks. A barge that can transport your kayak travels up and down the lake once a week, but you'll have to make advance arrangements. If you have use of a powerboat, you could easily launch it on the lake and make the 55 mile trip to the Stehekin landing yourself. This is also

Rainbow Creek Falls can be seen from the Stehekin River.

a good means if you want to take a dog; the *Lady of the Lake* doesn't take pets.

The *Lady of the Lake* does take rolled rafts, bundled paddles and lifejackets, and we've had two nice paddle-raft trips on the Stehekin. (There is a charge for baggage in excess of 70 pounds per paying passenger.) The boat runs from Chelan, at the southeast end of the lake, to the Stehekin landing, at the head of the lake, with several stops along the way to pick up or drop off hikers.

Catching the boat at the Fields Point landing, some 20 miles up the south shore of the lake, reduces the trip time by nearly an hour. Round trip from Fields Point to Stehekin in 1986 cost $17 per person and took about 3 hours, 30 minutes each way. In 1986 the *Lady of the Lake* left Fields Point at about 9:00 A.M. (be there at *least* half an hour early to get all your boating equipment out on the boat dock), arrived at the Stehekin landing at 12:30 P.M., left Stehekin at 2:00 P.M. and arrived back at Fields Point at 5:15 P.M.

Once you reach Stehekin landing, you have to get up the river. The Park Service operates shuttle vans ($2.00 each way to High Bridge; you'll need only a one-way ticket) that will carry you and your gear upriver. (The vans won't take kayaks or pets, however.) The Park Service shuttle doesn't leave until 2:00 P.M., so you have time to get organized and seek out the commercial rafters operating at the landing for a report on current river conditions. The Park Service usually has information on river conditions too.

Put-ins and Take-outs

Your shuttle van driver will usually be willing to make short detours along the way to see the sights, such as the 312 foot Rainbow Falls and a log cabin still in use as a one room schoolhouse.

If you're camping, I recommend a stop at Harlequin Campground on your way upriver to drop off your camping gear. Harlequin is below all of the rapids on the river, so on your way downriver you can stop and load all your gear in the boat without fear of waves getting it wet. Having your gear in the boat allows you to paddle down the lake to a beautiful, boat-access-only campground at Weaver Point. Before leaving home for a Stehekin trip, it's a good idea to pack so that you can quickly separate your camping gear so it can be dropped off at Harlequin.

After the stop at Harlequin, head upriver to your choice of two put-ins. The lower, more frequently used one (all of the commercial rafting trips use it) avoids the difficult rapids noted at the start of the log. It's located on an unmarked dirt turn-off toward the river about 0.3 of a mile below Bullion Camp; your driver should know where it is. The bank is fairly steep and the eddy small, but it's the best put-in on the upper river.

The upper put-in is even steeper and tougher. To reach it, continue upriver about 0.5 mile (well past Bullion Camp) to where the road begins to climb up and away from the river (High Bridge is so named because the bridge is high above the river which is in a tight gorge). You'll have to assemble your gear on the road and slide it down the rocks into the river. Park Service shuttle vans cannot drop you off at the upper put-in because there is no place to park.

Water Level

The Stehekin provides a fun trip between 1500 and 5000 cfs on the Stehekin gauge. Below 1,500 cfs you may have to drag your boat over many gravel bars. Above 5000 cfs the river is near flood stage and there are virtually no eddies. At flows above 3,500 cfs approach the part of the river above the lower put-in with great caution. It's very fast, has big holes and little opportunity to rescue anyone in the water.

Stehekin
Stehekin Gauge
Recommend 1,500 to 5,000 cfs

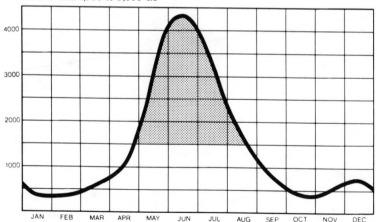

Special Hazards

Downed trees and logs are frequent hazards on the Stehekin, so stay alert. The river can also switch channels from year to year. Ask the Park Service or the commercial rafters at Stehekin landing about recent channel changes. In recent years, it has been necessary to take a small, new channel which you enter at about log time 1 hour, 25 minutes, by floating under a log across the channel.

Scenery

The scenery is some of the finest to be found on any eastern Washington river. Lake Chelan, an Indian name meaning "deep water" is 1,500 feet deep (placing the bottom 400 feet below sea level) and the deepest blue imaginable. It snakes between the towering, snow-capped crags of the North Cascades. The Stehekin valley, carpeted with beautiful, semi-open pine and fir forests, is flanked by mountain cliffs. From the green-tinged river you have beautiful views of the mountains and valley, including another chance to see the spectacular 312 foot Rainbow Falls.

MacGregor Mountain towers over the Stehekin valley,
at the head of Lake Chelan.

The upper river has lots of Class-2 action.

Camping

Camping on the lake is available at Weaver Campground. The Park Service shuttle provides access to campgrounds along the river at Harlequin and High Bridge.

Rapids

I've rated the Stehekin run intermediate because most boaters will want to start their trips at the lower put-in. **Cascade Rapids** can make a trip from the upper put-in an advanced or even expert run depending on the water level. Don't attempt to run **Cascade Rapids** until you have thoroughly scouted them from the bank.

From the lower put-in, all of the rapids are straightforward class 2 or less and should not present you with any problems.

If you'd like to look at some really crazy water, go to High Bridge and look at the stretch from High Bridge on up.

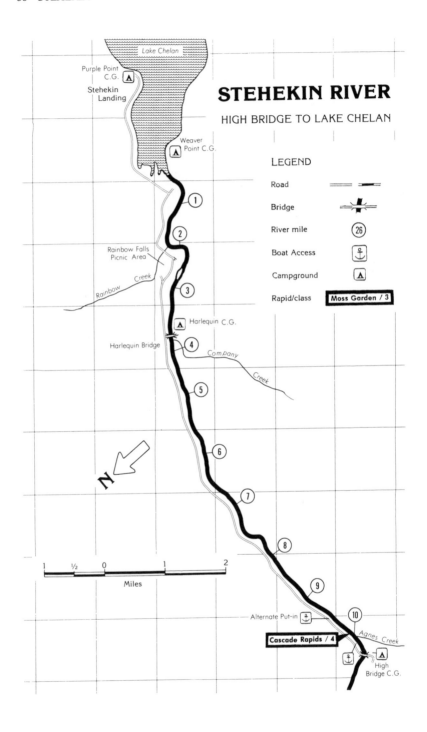

STEHEKIN RIVER

HIGH BRIDGE TO LAKE CHELAN

Lake Chelan

Purple Point C.G.

Stehekin Landing

Weaver Point C.G.

Rainbow Falls Picnic Area

Rainbow Creek

Harlequin C.G.

Harlequin Bridge

Company Creek

Alternate Put-in

Cascade Rapids / 4

Agnes Creek

High Bridge C.G.

LEGEND

Road	
Bridge	
River mile	(26)
Boat Access	
Campground	A
Rapid/class	Moss Garden / 3

N

1   ½   0   1   2
Miles

RIVER MILE	RIVER TIME	LEFT BANK	RAPIDS	RIGHT BANK	DESCRIPTION
	2:00				
	55				—Lake Chelan
	50				—Powerlines
	45				
	40				
	35				
	30				—Cable-car crossing
					—Remains of old bridge
	25				—Take left channel under log (right channel blocked)
	20				—Cable-car crossing
	15				—Blackberry Creek right
	10				—Rainbow Falls left (in distance)
	5				
	1:00				—Harlequin Bridge and Campground
	55				
RM 5	50		●2		
	45				—Powerlines
	40		●2		
	35		●2		
			●2		
	30		●2		
			●2		
	25		●2		
			●2		
	20		●2		
			●2		
	15		●2		—Coon Creek left
			●2		
	10		●2		
			●2		
			●3		
	5		●2		
			●3		
RM 10	12:00		●4		**Cascade Rapids,** scout left
					—Agnes Creek right

4

Elwha

Logged at - 1,500 cfs McDonald Bridge gauge
Recommended water level - 1,200 to 2,600 cfs
Best time - April through July
Rating - Intermediate
Water level information - NOAA Tape (206) 526-8530
NOAA Information (206) 526-6087
River mile - 13.4 to 7.5; 5.9 miles
Time - 1 hour, 22 minutes; 4.4 mph
Elevation - 400' to 205'; 32' per mile

Upper Elwha Dam to US 101

The Elwha provides summer boating in a very natural Olympic river valley with fine views of the surrounding mountains. Elwha means "elk" in the local Indian tongue and the valley is an important wintering place for the large Roosevelt elk. If you put in at Altaire Campground, you'll encounter rapids that are exciting but not very difficult. Above Altaire, **Gorge Rapids** is a challenge to the best of boaters.

Getting There
US 101 crosses the Elwha about seven miles west of Port Angeles.

Put-ins and Take-outs
The take-out is on the right bank just downstream of US 101, on land belonging to the Elwha Resort. The store owned by the resort is right along the highway. Ask at the store for permission to use the take-out.

To reach the put-in, take the road running up the east bank of the river into Olympic National Park. About one mile into the park the road is right along a bend in the river. Here is **Fisher-**

man's Bend, the most difficult rapid on the lower part of the river; you may want to scout it on the shuttle.

About 1.5 miles beyond **Fisherman's Bend,** the road crosses the river. Altaire Campground is to your right just beyond the bridge. The boat access area is at the downstream end of the campground.

If you wish to run the gorge, continue up the road beyond Altaire Campground. About 0.2 mile beyond the bridge over the river, an overgrown dirt road turns off to the left underneath the powerlines. Park on the main road, walk about 50 yards down the powerline access road and cut left to the river to get a look at *Gorge Rapids*. It's a nasty drop that has killed several people, mostly local people attempting to run the river with inadequate equipment.

To get to the upper put-in, continue up the main road. About 0.75 mile from the bridge over the river, you will come to a gravel road leading left, downhill to the powerhouse. A sign says "Private Road, Authorized Vehicles Only. No Camping." Park along the main road and carry your equipment about 200 yards down the gravel road to the river.

Water Level

The Elwha is a good trip between 1,200 and 2,600 cfs. Canoes and kayaks can probably scrape down on 800 cfs, but rafts would run aground. Over 2,600 cfs, there are very few eddies and rescue becomes difficult.

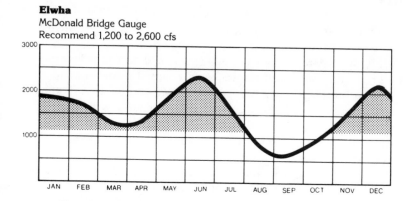

Elwha
McDonald Bridge Gauge
Recommend 1,200 to 2,600 cfs

Special Hazards

Logs in the Elwha frequently block some of the smaller channels between the numerous islands. Stick to the channels with the most water. **Gorge Rapids** is a very difficult rapid, approaching class 5 at some water levels. It should not be taken lightly and no one should run the upper portion of the river without scouting it first.

Scenery

The banks of the Elwha are heavily forested and you get many fine mountain views. The gorge just above the bridge near Altaire Campground is particularly pretty.

The deer and elk heavily affect the vegetation in the forest. This is graphically demonstrated on the left bank at log time 29 minutes. Land in the eddy there and walk back through the woods for 100 yards. There you'll find a small part of the forest fenced-off by a 12 foot high wire fence as an experiment. In contrast to the knee-high underbrush you have been walking through, the fenced-off area is choked with dense brush 15 feet high. In most of the forest each year, the deer and elk efficiently "mow" the underbrush.

Camping

Camping is plentiful in the Elwha valley. Just above Fisherman's Bend is Elwha Campground and just above the bridge is Altaire Campground. A fee is charged for camping at each.

Rapids

I rate this trip intermediate because most people will want to put in at Altaire Campgrounds. This trip is *not* intermediate if you run **Gorge Rapids,** then it is an expert trip.

The lower part of the river is all class 2 except for **Fisherman's Bend,** a straightforward class 3 easily scouted from the road.

Gorge Rapids is a real hair curler. Before you get to it, you have to run a substantial class 3 rapid, pock-marked with numerous big holes. Then you negotiate a sharp left bend, staying to the inside (left side) of a large rock in the middle of the channel. This brings you to **Gorge Rapids** proper.

Mid-way through the rapid is a large keeper hole extending out from the right bank two-thirds of the way across the river. Just below the hole is a large boulder, about one-third of the way out from the left bank.

A quarter of the water jams through a 2 foot wide slot to the left of the big boulder; there's no room there. How do you avoid the keeper hole on the right and get back to the right of the boulder?

The Elwha River flows through a steep, forested valley.

It's real tight. But you've got some help from a pillow wave which forms in front of the boulder. Rafts have to ride up on the wave, pull hard right and pivot to the right, running the bottom of the drop backward to make it. Kayakers will need a strong backferry to get through. Check it out, make your own plans, and if it looks too tough, put in at Altaire.

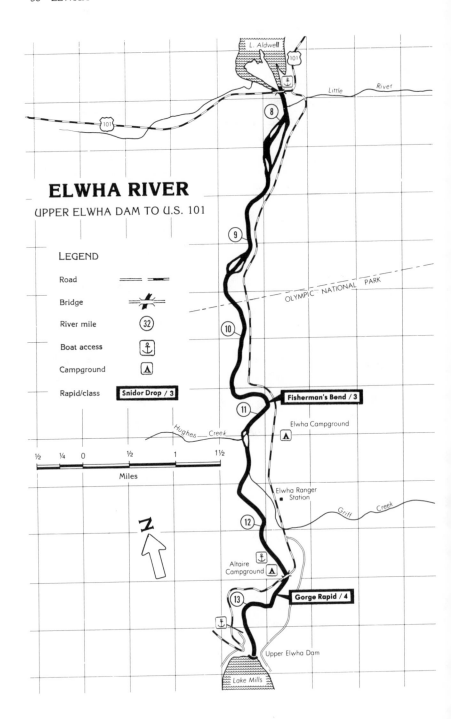

ELWHA RIVER
UPPER ELWHA DAM TO U.S. 101

LEGEND

Road	
Bridge	
River mile	32
Boat access	
Campground	
Rapid/class	Snidor Drop / 3

L. Aldwell

101

Little   River

8

OLYMPIC   NATIONAL   PARK

9

10

Fisherman's Bend / 3

11

Hughes   Creek

Elwha Campground

Elwha Ranger
Station

Griff   Creek

12

Altaire
Campground

Gorge Rapid / 4

13

Upper Elwha Dam

Lake Mills

½ ¼ 0   ½   1   1½

Miles

N

RIVER MILE	RIVER TIME	LEFT BANK	RAPIDS	RIGHT BANK	DESCRIPTION
	2:00				
	55				
	50				
	45				
	40				
	35				
	30				
	25				
	20			⚓	—Elwha Resort right
	15				—US 101 bridge / —Little River right
	10				
	5				—Gauging station with cable-car crossing / —Good playspot
	1:00		●2		
	55		●2		
	50		●2		—Good playspot / —Log across right channel / —Rock center-left
	45		●2		—Headwall left
	40		●3 ●3		—**Fishermen's Bend,** scout from road
	35		●2 ●2		—Hughes Creek left
	30		●2		—Eddy out left to see area fenced off from deer / —Good playspot at confluence
	25		●2		
	20		●2 ●2 ●2		—Large island with trees right
	15	⚓	●2 ●2		—Altaire Campground left / —Two islands with trees left
RM 10	10		●4 ●3		—**Gorge Drop,** scout from road, start left / —Run left of rock beyond powerline
	5		●2		—Run left of rock, shallow bar right
	12:00	⚓			—Powerhouse

Dry hillsides rise up and up from the Grande Ronde River.

5

Grande Ronde

Logged at -	7,000 cfs Troy gauge
Recommended water level -	1,500 to 9,000 cfs
Best time -	April to mid-July
Rating -	Advanced
Water level information -	NOAA Tape (206) 526-8530
	NOAA Information (206) 526-6087
	Portland River Forecast Center (503) 249-0666
River mile -	45.3 to 0: 45.3 miles
Time -	8 hours, 3 minutes; 5.8 mph
Elevation -	1585' to 815'; 17' per mile

Troy, Oregon to Snake River

The Grande Ronde provides Washington boaters with a southwestern United States style touring river. Here you'll find strange desert rock formations in a canyon over 3,000 feet deep. There is no road access to a portion of the run through a rugged canyon, making for pleasant picnicking and camping. The rapids are all class 1 or 2 difficulty, except for the Narrows, a series of three class 3 rapids near the end of the trip at river mile 4.5. The good beaches and generally sunny spring and summer weather make this a fine camping river. Bring sunscreen because the sun is intense.

The 44 mile trip upriver from this run (from Minam on the Wallowa river to Troy) is covered by John Garren in his guidebook, *Oregon River Tours*. Thus, between *Oregon River Tours* and this book, river logs for some 99 miles of the Wallowa and Grande Ronde rivers are available to the boater who would like to make the whole trip, which takes 4 to 7 days. The rapids on the stretch above Troy are class 2 and 3, and the river canyon is even more remote, with fine campsites.

The Grande Ronde has been the subject of several dam proposals in the 1970s and 1980s. The narrow canyon attracts hydroelectric developers. While none of these proposals is active now, they will undoubtedly be revived in the future. Get to know the Grande Ronde, *before* it is destroyed.

Getting There

The take-out is at Heller's Bar on the Snake River, 23 miles south of Asotin, which is 5 miles south of Clarkston. The road south of Asotin is paved for 14 miles, becoming gravel for the last 9 miles. At high water, the Snake sometimes floods the road, requiring either a drive through shallow water or complete closure of the road.

Washington State Route 129 stretches southwest into Oregon (becoming Oregon State Route 3) from Asotin. It is paved all the way and crosses the Grande Ronde at about river mile 26. Because of the depth of the river canyon, Route 129 winds down the steep slopes in many hairpin turns to the river.

Just south of the State Route 129 bridge over the river is a small cafe called the Oasis. The Oasis can arrange to shuttle your car from Troy to the Snake for you. The fare for the first car is $50 and each additional car is $35. It's best to make arrangements one week in advance. Call Carol or Duane at (509) 256-3372 or (509) 256-3375.

To reach Troy, take the gravel road which turns upstream off State Route 129 just north of the bridge over the river. It winds along the river bank some 29 miles to Troy.

Put-ins and Take-outs

The put-in is on the right bank, just downstream of the bridge across the river at Troy. Parking is scarce here; be sure that you don't block the access for others.

At the Oasis is another good put-in or take-out spot, to run either the easier upper part of the trip or the more difficult and remote lower part.

Besides the Heller's Bar take-out on the Snake, you can take out at a fishing access site on the left bank of the Grande Ronde at mile 2 or just above the bridge over the river at approximately mile 3. Both of these access points are equipped with sanicans. An advantage of these upper take-outs is that there is less chance that your car will be flooded; the Heller's Bar parking can be inundated when the Salmon River (a tributary to the Snake) rises in the spring run-off. Remember that you need a Department of Game access permit to park at fishing access sites.

Shuttling takes at least 1 hour, 45 minutes of hard driving, 65 miles one way. The route is not well signed, but generally follows the main roads in the area. From Heller's Bar, drive back downstream toward Asotin 10 miles, turn left on Asotin County Road No. 206, the Couse (pronounced "cows") Creek road. This one-lane gravel road snakes up a draw and winds around several hairpin turns to the top of the plateau above the river canyon.

On top of the plateau, continue another 5 miles on Road 206, which is now called the Montgomery Ridge Road, to State Route 129. It is 15 miles from the Snake to State Route 129. Turn left on State Route 129 and you will shortly reach Rattlesnake Summit (nearly 4,000 feet high) and begin the descent to the Grande Ronde. After winding down to the Grande Ronde, continue to Troy by turning right just before the bridge over the river. To run the shuttle the other way, watch for Montgomery Ridge Road, Road 206, off State Route 129 a little less than 2 miles beyond the turn-off to Fields Spring State Park.

Going into The Narrows

Water Level

The Grande Ronde is a nice trip between 1,500 and 9,000 cfs. Below 1,500 cfs you may run aground on some of the gravel bars and over 9,000 cfs the river approaches flood stage, eliminating most of the nice camping beaches. The water is much clearer and more attractive below 6,000 cfs. You should realize that the trip will take nearly twice as long at 1,500 cfs as it does at 7,000 cfs, the logged level.

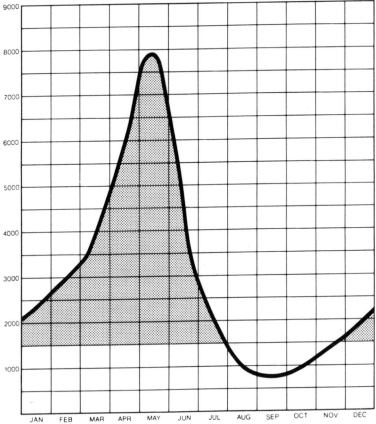

Grande Ronde
Troy Gauge
Recommend 1,500 to 9,000 cfs

Special Hazards

None other than the **Narrows**.

Scenery

Fifteen million years ago several volcanoes in the area of the Grande Ronde produced numerous lava flows. These flows built up the present-day plateau through which the river has cut a canyon over 3,000 feet deep. On the sides of the canyon you can see the different lava flows that stand out as giant stairs separated by layers of soil. More recent molten rock has been injected into the early lava flows, forming a series of basalt dikes called the Grande Ronde Dike Swarm. The dikes appear as strong, dark, resistant vertical streaks of rock. In some places the dikes stand up in erosional relief like great ruined walls.

The basalt dikes make for many spectacular rock formations, including some natural stone arches. The canyon for nine miles below the State Route 129 bridge is particularly narrow and beautiful. There is no road access to this section of the river and it is wonderful for picnicking and camping.

The Grande Ronde valley is generally too dry to support trees, a contrast to the pine forests along State Route 129, 3,000 feet above the river. A few semi-open pine forests occur in draws along the upper part of this run, but there are no forests in the lower part of

Coming out of The Narrows

Cattle and abandoned cabins are frequently seen along the banks.

the run. Small, scrub oaks along the lower part of the trip provide shade for camping.

Cattle from the many ranches along the river graze on the banks. They are particularly prevalent in the section above the State Route 129 bridge and between river miles 12 and 16. Otherwise, the scenery is quite natural.

Camping

Along the Grande Ronde are many beautiful and excellent campsites. The campsites shown on the log are all on benches above the river and therefore are available at high or low water. At water levels below 7,000 cfs, many other beach campsites would be possible. Much of the land along the river is in private hands and you may not camp without the owner's permission. All of the campsites on the log are on U. S. Bureau of Land Management land as best as I can determine. Locating boundary lines is difficult, however, since many of the lines have no fences. If you see anyone in the area, ask permission to camp. Often ranchers will allow camping on private land, if you ask. If you don't, you may well be run off with a shotgun.

Some planning in finding campsites is necessary since they are scarce in certain sections of the river. Generally, there are very few campsites away from the road in the section of the river above the State Route 129 bridge. Because of heavy ranching, campsites are also scarce between river miles 12 and 16 unless you get permission to camp on private land.

None of the water in the river or the tributaries is safe to drink. Bring your own water or purify the water with iodine or by sufficient boiling.

Rapids

The **Narrows** is the only significant rapid on this section of the Grande Ronde. This trip is rated advanced because of the **Narrows** and the isolation of the canyon below the State Route 129 bridge.

If you run your own shuttle, you can get a long-range look at the **Narrows** by driving up the road beyond the take-out. The road crosses from the north to the south side of the Grande Ronde at about river mile 3 and then winds over the ridge and up Joseph Creek (named for Chief Joseph of the Nez Perce). As the road starts up Joseph Creek, it is high above the river and, looking upstream, you can see the **Narrows** about a quarter of a mile away. Bring a pair of binoculars if you want to make much out.

The **Narrows** consists of three closely spaced class 3 drops around a gradual left bend in the river. At high water levels, you have to run all three drops at once because there is no place to eddy out between them. You can easily scout the drops from the left bank and portage light boats along the trail there (about 200 yards long).

There are numerous large waves and holes on the right side (outside of the bend) of the drops, but you can usually run down the middle as long as you meet the waves head on. At lower water levels, the river channel can narrow to a chute only 8 to 10 feet wide, forcing you to run right down the middle of the waves.

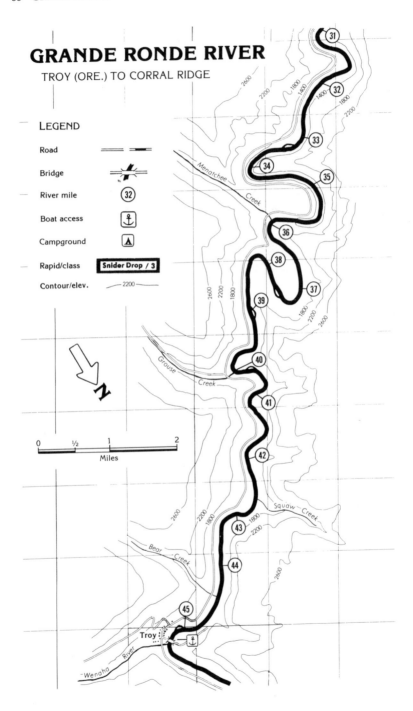

GRANDE RONDE RIVER

TROY (ORE.) TO CORRAL RIDGE

LEGEND

Road

Bridge

River mile

Boat access

Campground

Rapid/class   Snider Drop / 3

Contour/elev.   2200

N

0   ½   1   2
Miles

RIVER MILE	RIVER TIME	LEFT BANK	RAPIDS	RIGHT BANK	DESCRIPTION
	2:00				—McNeill Island
	55				—Powerline
	50				
	45				
RM 35	40				
	35				
	30				—Menatchee Creek left
	25				
	20				
	15				
	10				
	5				—Road sign left 35 MPH
	1:00				
	55				
RM 40	50				—Grouse Creek left
	45				
	40		2		
	35				—Old barn right
	30				—Squaw Creek right
	25				—Old barn left
	20				—Powerline
	15				
	10				—Bear Creek left
RM 45	5				—Gauging station and cable-car crossing followed by powerlines
	12:00				—Troy bridge
					—Wenaha River left

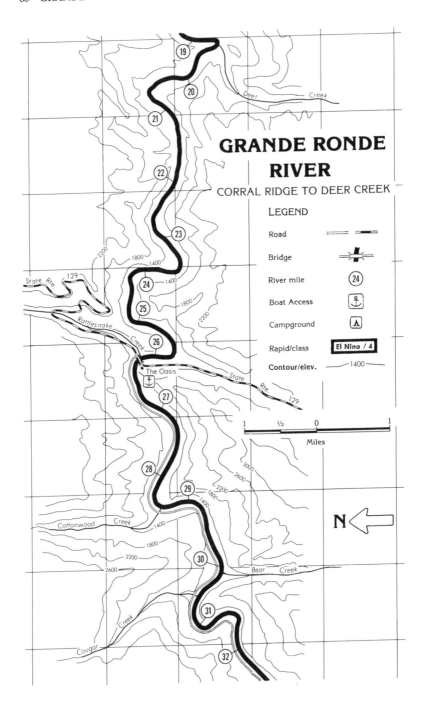

GRANDE RONDE RIVER

CORRAL RIDGE TO DEER CREEK

LEGEND

Road	
Bridge	
River mile	(24)
Boat Access	
Campground	
Rapid/class	El Nino / 4
Contour/elev.	1400

RIVER MILE	RIVER TIME	LEFT BANK	RAPIDS	RIGHT BANK	DESCRIPTION
	4:00		▬		—Rock buttress right
	55				
	50				
	45	☼	☼		—Huge boulder on right side of river channel, steeple rock on cliff left
	40			☼	—Natural rock arch high on right
	35	☼	❘		—Natural rock arch high on left
RM 25	30		❘ ●2		
	25	🏠			—Hay shed left
	20	🏠	❘		—Powerline
	15			⚓	—State Route 129 bridge / The Oasis, Rattlesnake Creek left
	10			🏠	
	5	🏠			—Large hay shed left
	3:00	⛺			—Game Department campground left
	55			⛺	
	50				—Cottonwood Creek left
	45		❘		
	40				
RM 30	35	🏠	❘		
	30			⛺	—Bear Creek right
		⚓			—Cable-car crossing
	25				—Department of Game fishing access left / Cougar Creek left
	20				—Powerlines
		⛺			
	15			⛺	—Powerlines / Cable-car crossing
	10	🏠			—Large shed left
	5				
	2:00				

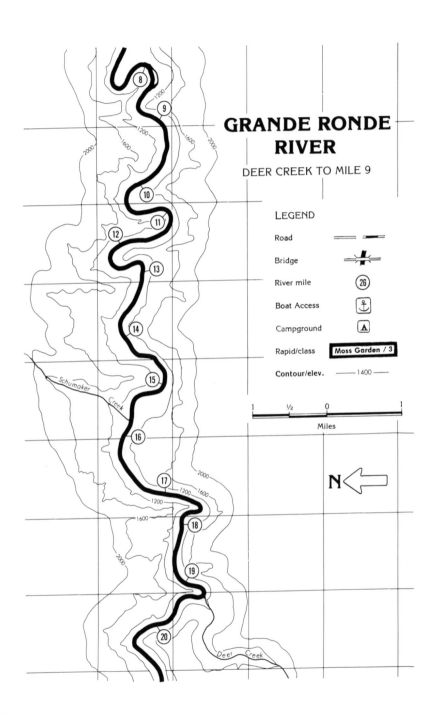

GRANDE RONDE RIVER

DEER CREEK TO MILE 9

LEGEND

Road	
Bridge	
River mile	26
Boat Access	⚓
Campground	▲
Rapid/class	Moss Garden / 3
Contour/elev.	—— 1400 ——

Miles

N

RIVER MILE	RIVER TIME	LEFT BANK	RAPIDS	RIGHT BANK	DESCRIPTION
	6:00				
	55				
	50				
	45				
	40				—Old cabin and shed left
	35				
	30				—Rock buttress right
	25				
	20				—Headwall right
	15				
RM 15	10				—Cable ferry
					Schumaker Creek left, followed by
	5				—cable-crossings
					—Powerlines
	5:00				—Barn left
	55				—Pinnacle rock on bluff left
	50				
	45				
	40				
	35				—Abandoned red house right
	30				—Cable-car crossing
	25				—Abandoned homestead right
	20				—Deer Creek right
					—Rock buttress left
RM 20	15				
	10		•2		—Big waves
	5				
	4:00				

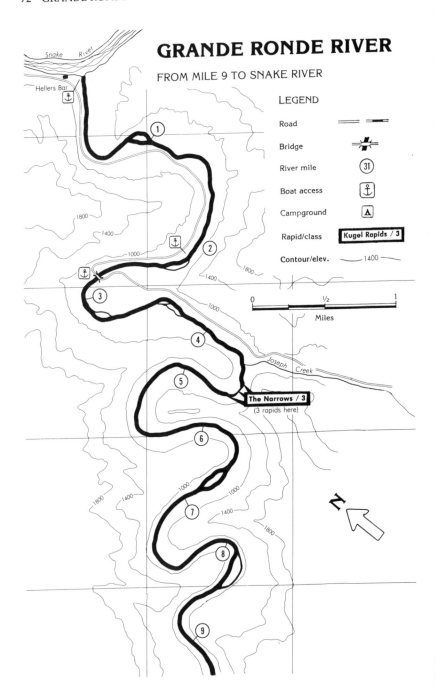

GRANDE RONDE RIVER

FROM MILE 9 TO SNAKE RIVER

LEGEND

Road	
Bridge	
River mile	31
Boat access	⚓
Campground	A
Rapid/class	Kugel Rapids / 3
Contour/elev.	1400

Snake River

Hellers Bar

The Narrows / 3
(3 rapids here)

Joseph Creek

0   ½   1
Miles

N

RIVER MILE	RIVER TIME	LEFT BANK	RAPIDS	RIGHT BANK	DESCRIPTION
RM 0	8:00	⚓			—Heller's Bar left —Confluence with Snake River
	55				
	50				
	45		•2		
	40				
	35	⚓			Powerlines followed by Game —Department access left —Hay shed right
	30		•2		
	25	⚓			—Game Department fishing access left
	20				—Powerlines
	15		•2		—Joseph Creek right
	10		●3 ●3		—**The Narrows**, scout left
RM 5	5				—Powerlines
	7:00	⌂			
	55	⌂			
	50				
	45				
	40				
	35	⌂			
	30				—Large island with trees —Small cabin right
	25			⌂	
	20				
	15				
RM 10	10				—Scenic cliffs left
	5	⌂		⌂	
	6:00				

6

Logged at - 1,300 cfs Randle Gauge
Recommended water level - 1,200 to 2,800 cfs (varies)
Best time - April through early July
Rating - Advanced
Water level information - NOAA Tape (206) 526-8530
NOAA Information (206) 526-6087
River mile - 64.7 to 59.2; 5.5 miles
Time - 1 hour, 30 minutes; 3.7 mph
Elevation - 1155' to 1015'; 25' per mile

Rush Creek to Eagle Cliff Bridge

A trip on the Lewis provides you with gorgeous scenery, including one of the most beautiful sights on any Washington river: Curly Creek Falls. Curly Creek drops 60 feet in a thundering cascade into the Lewis through two natural stone arches. You can paddle or row your boat right under the falls in a setting that seems to be right out of a Tarzan movie. The mist from the falls keeps the area lush in spectacular greenery. The trip is short, with moderate whitewater, but well worth making for the scenery. The Lewis is named for A. Lee Lewis who homesteaded near its mouth.

Getting There

Take exit 21 from I-5 at Woodland and follow State Route 503 some 31 miles east to Cougar. This town's name was selected from a list of animals submitted by townspeople to the Postal Service. Cougar is famous as the place where D. B. Cooper bailed out of an airliner following the first skyjacking of modern times.

From Cougar continue east on the U. S. Forest Service 90 road

Curly Creek Falls (note the two natural stone arches)

Rigging a boat near the mouth of Rush Creek

some 20 miles to the Pine Creek Information Station. Shortly beyond the Information Station the 90 road turns to the right to Eagle Cliff Bridge.

Put-ins and Take-outs

The take-out is just below the bridge on the right hand side.

To reach the put-in, continue across the bridge and up the 90 road approximately 4.5 miles to where the 51 road turns off to the right toward Carson. About 0.95 mile beyond the intersection you will cross a bridge over Rush Creek (signed). Another 0.15 mile beyond the bridge, turn downhill toward the river on an unsigned dirt road. The road switch-backs 0.8 mile to a point near Rush Creek, where you bear right onto the branch that turns upriver 0.15 mile and ends at the put-in. From the put-in, you'll want to ferry across the river passing to the right of a gravel bar in the center of the river.

For an alternate put-in, turn off the 90 road onto Forest Service road 9039. This road turns off the 90 road about 4.3 miles from Eagle Cliff Bridge or about 0.2 mile short of the intersection with the 51 road. Approximately 0.8 mile down this road you will cross the river on the bridge which appears at log time 29 minutes. The put-in trail on the upper side of the bridge on the right bank is steep, but not too difficult.

Kayakers may wish to consider a put-in much farther upriver where the 90 road crosses the river near Cussed Hollow. This is near river mile 71, making the trip about 12 miles. This portion of the river is very beautiful with no signs of civilization. The water is mostly class 2–3 with two difficult stretches. The first is at a sharp left bend in the river, just beyond a small creek entering on the left, a little over 2 miles into the trip. Here is class 4 at most water levels but can be read easily. The other difficult stretch comes about 2 miles farther, just above the mouth of Big Creek. Here the river rushes through a tight gorge filled with huge boulders. Since the gaps between the boulders are often no more than 4 to 5 feet wide, this gorge is impassable to rafts (with the possible exception of small paddle rafts). Kayakers, however, may be able to run the gaps or else carry their boats around the 200 yard gorge on the trail on the right bank.

Water Level

No gauge on the Lewis gives current water level reports. There is a gauge, however, at Randle on the Cispus, which is the next drainage to the north. This gauge provides a reasonably accurate measure of conditions on the Lewis. The Cispus drains more high snowfields than the Lewis and therefore has more summer flow than the Lewis. Flows in the Lewis amount to the following percentages of flow in the Cispus: January and February: 123%, March and April, 94%; May, 83%; June, 75%; July, 64%; August, 82%; September, 74%; and October through December, 102%.

These percentages translate into the following recommended minimum and maximum water levels for the Lewis:

	Jan–Feb	Mar–Apr	May	June	July	Aug	Sept	Oct–Dec
Min	750	1000	1100	1200	1400	1100	1200	900
Max	1600	2100	2600	2800	3000	2500	2800	2000

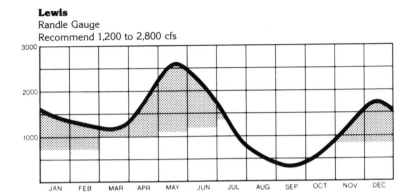

Lewis
Randle Gauge
Recommend 1,200 to 2,800 cfs

Special Hazards

Many logs clutter the Lewis at high water. The positions of the log jams change from year to year and you should keep a sharp lookout for logs blocking the channel.

Scenery

The scenery on this trip is magnificent. Besides Curly Creek Falls, which is worth the trip by itself, there is the smaller Miller Creek Falls just downstream and a beautiful, tight gorge extending approximately from river mile 63 to 62. The whole trip above river mile 61 is quite natural, with the bridge as the only sign of civilization. Unfortunately, clearcuts come into view below mile 61. This land was clearcut and not replanted in the late 1960s when Pacific Power and Light planned a huge dam at Eagle Cliff, the take-out. This project, which would inundate the logged run, is not dead—only placed on hold until economics permit completion. Support Wild & Scenic protection of the Lewis to prevent destruction of this beautiful river.

The shuttle provides views of Mt. St. Helens, and paddlers may wish to take a side trip to view Lower Falls on the Lewis upriver from the trip described here. The Lewis plummets 35 feet in a spectacular curtain of whitewater just downstream from Lower Falls Campground, located about 1.5 miles beyond the bridge over the river at Cussed Hollow on the 90 road.

Camping

Camping is plentiful. There are campgrounds at Lower Falls, Swift Camp (about 1.5 miles west of the ranger station) and at Beavertail Recreation Area (about 1 mile east of Cougar).

Rapids

The most difficult rapid of the logged trip is **Eagle Cliff Drop,** which can be easily inspected from the take-out. The river below Rush Creek is a fairly easy whitewater trip, but has some good playspots and beautiful scenery.

There's a good playspot near the bridge at the take-out.

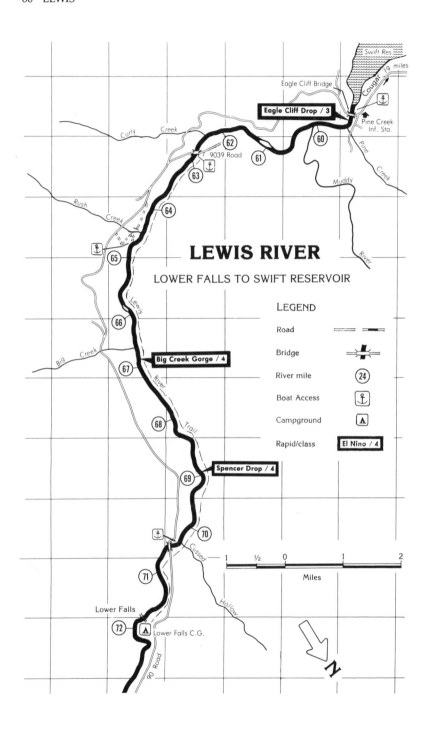

LEWIS RIVER

LOWER FALLS TO SWIFT RESERVOIR

Eagle Cliff Drop / 3

Big Creek Gorge / 4

Spencer Drop / 4

Lower Falls

Lower Falls C.G.

LEGEND

Road	
Bridge	
River mile	24
Boat Access	
Campground	
Rapid/class	El Nino / 4

Swift Res

Cougar 19 miles

Eagle Cliff Bridge

Pine Creek Inf. Sta.

Pine Creek

Muddy River

Curly Creek

9039 Road

Rush Creek

Lewis River

Big Creek

River Trail

Cussed Hollow

90 Road

Miles

N

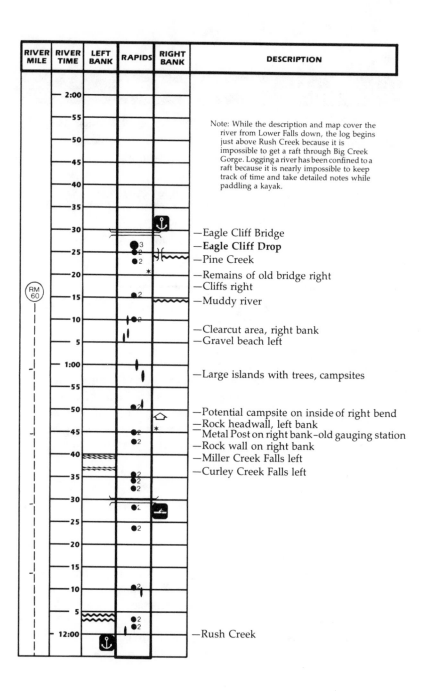

RIVER MILE	RIVER TIME	LEFT BANK	RAPIDS	RIGHT BANK	DESCRIPTION
	2:00				
	55				
	50				Note: While the description and map cover the river from Lower Falls down, the log begins just above Rush Creek because it is impossible to get a raft through Big Creek Gorge. Logging a river has been confined to a raft because it is nearly impossible to keep track of time and take detailed notes while paddling a kayak.
	45				
	40				
	35				
	30			⚓	—Eagle Cliff Bridge
	25		●3 ●2		**Eagle Cliff Drop**
			●2		—Pine Creek
	20		*		—Remains of old bridge right
RM 60	15		●2		—Cliffs right
					—Muddy river
	10		┃●2		
	5		┃┃		—Clearcut area, right bank
					—Gravel beach left
	1:00		┃ ┃		
	55				—Large islands with trees, campsites
	50		●2		
				⬦	—Potential campsite on inside of right bend
	45		●2 *		—Rock headwall, left bank
			●2		—Metal Post on right bank–old gauging station
	40	〜〜			—Rock wall on right bank
		〜〜			—Miller Creek Falls left
	35		●2 ●2		—Curley Creek Falls left
			●2		
	30	⌒	●2	◼	
	25		●2		
	20				
	15				
	10		●2 ┃		
	5	〜〜〜	●2		
	12:00		●2 ┃		—Rush Creek
		⚓			

7

Upper Soleduck

Logged at - 1,400 cfs McDonald Bridge gauge
Recommended water level - 1,200 to 3,000 cfs (varies)
Best time - April to mid-June
Rating - Advanced
Water level information - NOAA Tape (206) 526-8530
NOAA Information (206) 526-6087
River mile - 53.8 to 29.9; 23.9 miles
Time - 7 hours, 19 minutes; 3.3 mph
Elevation - 1020' to 330'; 29' per mile

Fibreboard Bridge to Salmon Hatchery

The Upper Soleduck provides interesting rapids on a rain forest odyssey. The rapids are not difficult at the moderate water levels found in spring and summer, but they enliven one of the most beautiful river trips in Washington. There are lush, moss covered forests, abundant wildlife, breath-taking gorges and crystalline water in a boulder studded channel. This trip is also long enough to provide a nice overnight for those who are not afraid to risk camping in the rain.

Getting There
The Soleduck is paralleled by US 101 about 30 miles west of Port Angeles.

Put-ins and Take-outs
To reach the upper put-in, turn off of US 101 on the South Fork Soleduck road (Forest Service road 2918). The road leaves US 101 4.7 miles west of the west end of Lake Crescent or about 0.4 mile east of mile marker No. 216. The upper put-in is at the bridge (known as the Fibreboard Bridge) over the Soleduck about 3 miles up the South Fork Soleduck road.

Riding the waves at the bottom of Snider Drop

For an alternative put-in turn right off the South Fork Soleduck road about 0.95 mile from US 101 on an unmarked dirt road. Drive about 0.1 mile to the river where you start your trip at log time 39 minutes. This put-in has the advantage of being below two of the three spots where water may be insufficient because the river braids around several islands.

The next potential put-in or take-out is at Klahowya Forest Service Camp. From US 101 turn in at the campground and bear to the left around the one-way road. At the last campground (the farthest downstream) you will find an unimproved boat ramp. This appears at log time 2 hours, 53 minutes.

The next potential put-in or take-out is at a place known locally as Riverside. It is just a rough spot over the bank next to a wide asphalt turnout along US 101, just west of a sign (facing west) saying Slow Vehicles Use Turnouts Next 15 miles. The sign is 0.8 mile west of the bridge over the river near Klahowya Campground or, coming from the west, 1.5 miles east of an Olympic National Forest sign. Riverside appears on the log at time 3 hours, 8 minutes.

The Bear Creek boat ramp is a favorite put-in or take-out of fishermen for their drift boats. To reach the boat ramp, turn off US 101 on an unmarked dirt road opposite the Bear Creek Tavern. The

Hole-riding in Water Garden

turn-off is 0.3 mile east of the bridge on US 101 over Bear Creek. About 0.2 mile down the dirt road you will reach the boat ramp marked by a sign warning Extreme Danger, Hazardous Rapids Downstream, Washington Game Department.

The last take-out on the run is at the salmon hatchery below Sappho. The turn-off to the hatchery leaves US 101 where the road cuts off a bend in the river, about 0.2 mile from a bridge from either direction. Immediately after taking the turn-off to the south, you should turn right, in the direction marked by a small white Hatchery sign. Drive about 1.5 miles downriver to the hatchery; the boat ramp is to your right. There is also a dam just above the boat ramp, and you may wish to take out above it.

Water Level

No gauge has up-to-date reports on the Soleduck, so the water level must be judged by the gauge on the Elwha, the next basin over. The Elwha gauge provides a fairly good indication of conditions on the Soleduck, but certainly not an exact measurement.

Lots of boulders stud the heavily forested path of the Soleduck.

The Elwha gets more snow run-off than the Soleduck, so a higher reading is needed on the McDonald Bridge gauge later in the season than early on. What you are looking for is a somewhat greater than average flow in the spring. It is usually present after a good rain or after a couple days of hot weather that melts the snow. Recommended minimum and maximum levels for the Soleduck in spring are as follows:

	April	May 1–15	May 16–31	June 1–15	June 16–on
minimum	1,200	1,500	1,800	2,100	2,400
maximum	2,400	3,000	3,600	3,700	3,900

You have to use some good sense in making use of this table. It is based upon average weather conditions. For example, in early May, if it has been colder and wetter than normal, look at the April figures. If it has been hotter and drier than normal, however, look at the late May figures. Also note that these are the recommended boating levels; you can scrape down the river with a lot less. Fishermen regularly take their drift boats down the Soleduck at least through mid-June every year, but they're looking for good fishing, not good boating.

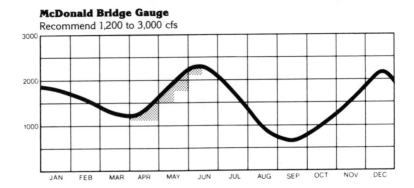

Special Hazards

Fishermen are not really a special hazard, but remember that they were here first. Stay out of the way of their lines, particularly if they have a fish on. Fishing season usually lasts from winter through March and begins again in late May, continuing through July. The part of the river open to fishing can vary from year to year, but generally the Upper Soleduck is not open above Klahowya Campground, thus it's a good area to boat during fishing season.

A difficulty, though not much of a hazard, is that in the uppermost part of the river are several places where the river braids around islands leaving none of the several channels with enough water to boat. This problem requires a short portage over a boulder bar, or at least some pushing and sliding of your boat over the rocks. Using the put-in at log time 39 minutes avoids two of three particularly bad spots. They are located at log times 13 minutes, 28 minutes, and 52 minutes.

The Washington State Department of Fisheries has constructed a dam across the river just above the boat ramp at the salmon hatchery in order to divert water for the hatchery. A boat slot cut in the dam, on the right side, is where you should go over the dam to avoid damage to your boat.

Scenery

Although paralleled by roads, the upper part of this run seems quite remote. It presents a fantasy of greenery: deep green ferns, luxuriant mosses and bright new shoots blend into a study of green, accentuated by the brown of the trees and rocks. Between the rapids are many deep, clear pools where salmon and steelhead can be seen. Bald eagles come to the Soleduck for the fish and I've seen them every time I've boated the upper part of the river.

The river has cut its own narrow channel, which lies about 30 feet below the level of the surrounding valley. Its heavily forested slopes screen out most evidence of civilization. A trip on the Soleduck is the best way to enjoy the rain forest.

Camping

Klahowya Campground, at log time 2 hours, 45–55 minutes, provides many beautiful campsites with views of the river. Open year-round.

The State DNR Wahlgren Memorial Campground, open throughout the year, is above the river on the right bank at log time 5 hours, 23–28 minutes. It is not visible from the river but provides campsites with picnic tables and fire pits. It is about three miles east of the turn-off to the salmon hatchery, just a little downriver from the turn-off to the Bear Creek boat-ramp.

Campsites provided by ITT Rayonier are available in the Tumbling Rapids Recreation Area right across US 101 from the turn-off to the salmon hatchery. Tumbling Rapids is usually open only from Memorial Day weekend through Labor Day, however.

For those who would like to make this an overnight trip, potential campsites on public property are indicated on the log. Nearly all of the land on the left bank of the river is owned by government agencies and you can camp there if you do a little scouting first to make sure that you are not near someone's house.

Rapids

Although this trip has a good number of class 2 and 3 rapids, its primary attraction is the scenery rather than the whitewater. The drops provide many good playspots and put a little excitement in the trip, but are fairly widely spaced. The last part of this trip, known to fishermen as the Bear Creek stretch, offers the only sustained rapids of the trip. Most of the rapids are boulder gardens, requiring technical maneuvering, rather than big drops with large waves. The biggest rapid of the trip, **Snider Drop,** provides a long technical rock dodge, followed by a good drop at the end.

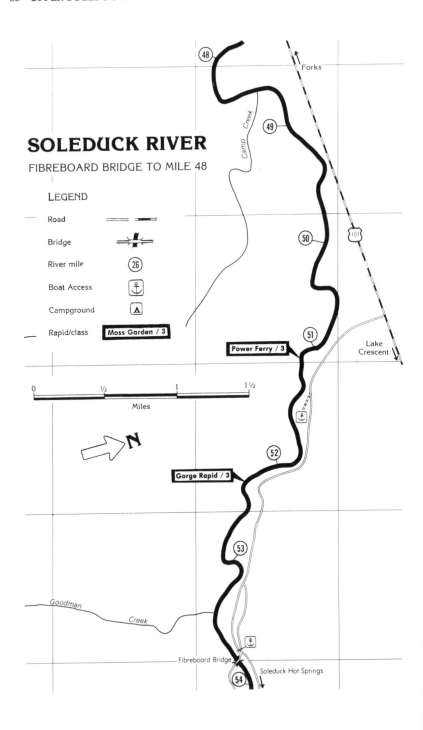

SOLEDUCK RIVER

FIBREBOARD BRIDGE TO MILE 48

LEGEND

Road	
Bridge	
River mile	(26)
Boat Access	
Campground	
Rapid/class	Moss Garden / 3

0   ½   1   1½
Miles

N

Forks

Camp Creek

Power Ferry / 3

Lake Crescent

Gorge Rapid / 3

Goodman Creek

Fibreboard Bridge

Soleduck Hot Springs

RIVER MILE	RIVER TIME	LEFT BANK	RAPIDS	RIGHT BANK	DESCRIPTION
	2:00				
	55		●3		
	50		☼		—Large rock, center channel
	45				
	40	〰			—Camp Creek left
	35				
	30		●2		
	25		●2	▬ ⊓	—Mobile home —Cook-out pavillion
	20		●2		
	15	〰	●3		—Channel right, near bushes
	10			⬟	—Shed right
	5		〽		—Huge rock right, next to large eddy
	1:00			⬟	—A-frame cabin right
	55	▮	●2		—20-foot-high rock walls left
			●3 ▮ ▮		—Good playspot
	50		●3		—**Power Ferry,** good playspot
	45				
	40		●2	⚓	
	35		●2 ●2	▪	—Grey rock wall right
	30	⊟	●3 ▮	⊟	—**Gorge Rapid**
	25		●2		
	20				
	15	〳	●2 ▮		—Downed trees between islands
	10				
	5	〰	●2	⬠	—Goodman Creek left
	12:00	≈		⚓	—Fibreboard Bridge, South Fork Soleduck Road

RM 50

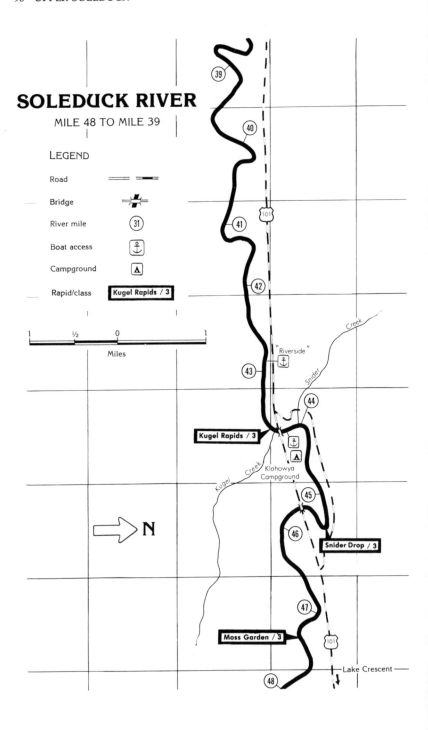

SOLEDUCK RIVER

MILE 48 TO MILE 39

LEGEND

Road	
Bridge	
River mile	③①
Boat access	⚓
Campground	⛺
Rapid/class	**Kugel Rapids / 3**

Miles

N

③⑨

④⓪

101

④①

④②

Creek

"Riverside" ⚓

Snider

④③

④④

Kugel Rapids / 3 ⚓

⛺

Kugel Creek

Klahowya Campground

④⑤

④⑥

Snider Drop / 3

④⑦

Moss Garden / 3

101

Lake Crescent

④⑧

RIVER MILE	RIVER TIME	LEFT BANK	RAPIDS	RIGHT BANK	DESCRIPTION
	4:00				—Mobile home left
	55				
RM 40	50		•2		
	45		•2		
	40		•2		
	35		•2		—Powerlines, mobile home left
			•2		
	30				
	25		•2		
	20				
	15		•2		
	10		•2		
			•2		
	5		•2		—Riverside
			•2		
	3:00		❘●3		**Kugel Rapids**
	55				—Kugel Creek left
					—Highway bridge
					—Klahowya Campground boat-ramp
	50		•2		—Snider Creek right
					—Mobile homes and heavy equipment right
	45		•2		—Klahowya Campground left
	40				
RM 45	35				
	30		●3		—Rock wall right
					—Snider Drop
	25				—Highway bridge
					—Logs block channel right
	20				
	15		•2		
	10		•2		
			•2		
	5		●3		**—Moss Garden**
	2:00				

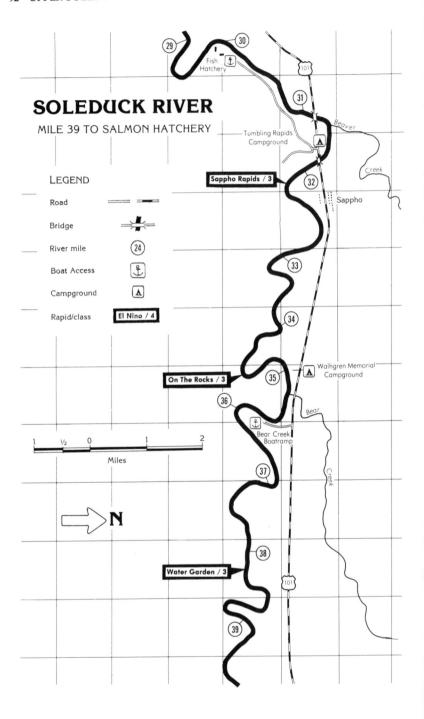

SOLEDUCK RIVER

MILE 39 TO SALMON HATCHERY

LEGEND

Road	
Bridge	
River mile	(24)
Boat Access	
Campground	A
Rapid/class	El Nino / 4

Fish Hatchery

Tumbling Rapids Campground

Sappho Rapids / 3

Sappho

On The Rocks / 3

Walhgren Memorial Campground

Bear Creek Boatramp

Water Garden / 3

Beaver Creek

Bear Creek

Miles

N

RIVER MILE	RIVER TIME	LEFT BANK	RAPIDS	RIGHT BANK	DESCRIPTION
	6:00		•2		
	55				
	50		•3		—Cable-car crossing
	45		•2 •2 •3		
	40				
	35		•3 •3		—Channel far right —**On the Rocks,** channel far right
RM 35	30		•2		—Salmon hatchery outlet with controlling structure left
	25				—Fish-rearing facilities and outlet left
	20				—Powerlines
	15				—Bear Creek right
	10		•2 •2		—Good playspot
	5		•2		—Bear Creek boat-ramp
	5:00				
	55				
	50		•2		
	45		•2		—Rock walls right, deep pool
	40				
	35		•2		
	30				
	25				
	20		•3 •3		—**Water Garden,** good playspot
	15		•2 •2		
	10		•2		
	5				
	4:00		•2		—Powerlines

There's lots of rock dodging on the Soleduck.

RIVER MILE	RIVER TIME	LEFT BANK	RAPIDS	RIGHT BANK	DESCRIPTION
	8:00				
	55				
	50				
	45				
	40				
	35				
	30				
	25				
	20				
	15				
	10				
	5				
RM 30	7:00				
	55				—Salmon hatchery pumping tower
	50				
	45				—Powerlines
	40				—Highway bridge
	35				
	30		●2		—Beaver Creek right
	25				—Tumbling Rapids Recreation Area left
					—Highway bridge
	20		●3		—**Sappho Rapids**
			* ●2		—Remains of old bridge left
	15				—Islands across river, run gaps
	10				
	5		●3		
	6:00				

8

Lower Cispus

Logged at - 1,500 cfs on Randle gauge
Recommended water level - 1,400 to 3,500 cfs
Best time - April to early July
Rating - Advanced
Water level information - NOAA Tape (206) 526-8530
NOAA Information (206) 526-6087
U. S. Geological Survey (206) 593-6510
River mile - 16.6 to Cowlitz mile 89.4; 17.1 miles
Time - 3 hours, 48 minutes; 4.5 mph
Elevation - 1265′ to 815′; 26′ per mile

Road 28 Bridge to Cowlitz Falls

The Cispus is a relatively little-known whitewater run in Gifford Pinchot National Forest. It has very enjoyable class 2 to 3 rapids at moderate water levels, pretty scenery and a fairly long season. If you connect this lower run with the upper part of the river, it provides the longest whitewater run in Washington State: nearly 30 miles of excitement. As mentioned in the chapter on the Upper Cispus, it would make a great overnight trip with a camp along the river, if a channel could be kept free of logs.

The Army Corps of Engineers would like to study the feasibility of building a large hydroelectric dam on the Cispus. Called the Greenhorn Creek Project, this dam would inundate all of this trip above Iron Creek. If you would like to save the Cispus, contact Friends of Whitewater, listed in the Preface, and help make the Cispus a federally protected Wild & Scenic River.

Left: Top—Lots of logs line the bank during the first part of the trip.
Center—Hold on in Roller Coaster.
Bottom—Much of the Lower Cispus is heavily forested.

Getting There

The Cispus is usually approached through the town of Randle on U. S. 12. Randle is about 54 miles east of I-5 and has a Forest Service Ranger Station. From the Puget Sound area north of Tacoma, the fastest way to Randle is on State Route 7, south through Spanaway, LaGrande and Morton to U. S. 12.

Put-ins and Take-outs

To reach the put-in from Randle, take the Forest Service 23 road south toward Trout Lake. You'll cross the Cowlitz just after leaving Randle and, in about 1.0 mile, bear left toward the Cispus Environmental Center and Trout Lake. After driving about 10 miles through beautiful forest, turn right onto the 28 road which crosses the Cispus toward the Environmental Center. Put-in on the left bank, downstream from the bridge.

A put-in or take-out can also be made at Tower Rock Campground at river mile 15.7 or at Iron Creek Campground at river mile 8. An alternative to the Iron Creek Campground is about 1.0 mile upriver at the beach marked on the log at time 1 hour, 52 minutes. The river guides refer to this place as the "twin cedars" due to the two large trees there.

Another possible put-in or take-out point is at the mouth of Greenhorn Creek, reached at the end of the Forest Service 044 road. This 0.2 mile long gravel road is not well marked, but turns off of the Greenhorn 76 road that runs along the south side of the Cispus, a little downriver from where the 77 road turns off.

A put-in or take-out could also be made at Huffaker Bridge at river mile 7 or at the bridge near river mile 4.5, though the bank is quite steep in both places. The bridges, the mouth of Greenhorn Creek, and both Tower Rock and Iron Creek campgrounds can be reached along the south side of the river. From the put-in, head south on the 28 road. Just beyond where the road crosses Yellowjacket Creek Bridge (0.9 mile from the put-in) turn right onto the Greenhorn 76 road. In 0.7 mile, bear right toward the Trout Farm. In 0.3 mile, a right turn will take you to Tower Rock Campground and a left will allow you to continue on the 76 road on the south bank of the Cispus. About 3 miles farther (just beyond the intersection with the 77 road) the pavement ends and the road becomes gravel. The gravel road continues about another 3.5 miles until the bridge over Iron Creek.

To get to the lower take-outs, cross the river on the Huffaker Bridge on the 25 road at about river mile 7. Drive north a little over

Tower Rock dominates the view at the put-in.

1 mile and make a sharp left on an unmarked dirt road and continue down the north bank. This will take you to the bridge at
river mile 4.5 and to the new take-out at the upper end of the
reservoir which will form behind the future Cowlitz Falls dam. In
time for the 1989 or 1990 boating season, a new take-out will be in-
stalled just a little below river mile 2. Lewis County PUD should
be beginning construction on the Cowlitz Falls dam by then. The

dam will back up the Cispus to river mile 1.7, forcing a take-out here to avoid the reservoir. When the take-out is developed, it will be marked with a sign.

Through the 1988 season, it should be possible to take out just above Cowlitz Falls on the Cowlitz. The last 0.3 mile of the run on the Cowlitz has two fun rapids and beautiful scenery, which will be lost to the Cowlitz Falls project. To reach the take-out just above the falls, you have to go back through Randle (the wooden bridge over the Cowlitz that ran from the road on the north bank of the Cispus collapsed into the river in 1986 and there are no plans to rebuild it).

From Randle, go west on US 12 about 11 miles and turn left on the Kosmos road. In about 100 yards, bear left on the Green River 27 road. This road runs along the shore of Riffe Lake for about three miles. As the 27 road leaves the lake shore, turn left on a wide gravel road. This road runs straight more than 2 miles. After 2 miles, bear right at the intersection onto Falls Road. This road winds back around a mountain and reaches a boat ramp on the Cowlitz in about 0.75 mile.

Water Level

The Cispus is an enjoyable class 2 to 3 run at a wide variety of water levels. Above 3,000 cfs some of the class 3 rapids can develop powerful hydraulics, approaching class 4. A large whirlpool forms at the confluence of the Cispus and the Cowlitz at levels over 3,500 cfs, so I suggest that you take out above the confluence at high water. You can bump your way down the river with as little as 1,000 cfs, but the ride is much more enjoyable with at least 1,400 cfs.

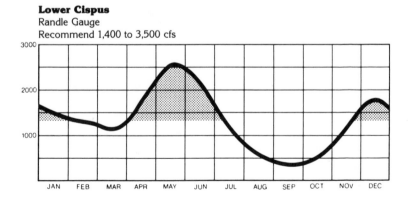

Lower Cispus
Randle Gauge
Recommend 1,400 to 3,500 cfs

Special Hazards

A number of logs on this part of the Cispus can form jams along the outside of river bends. Rarely, however, will they block the main river channel, but keep alert!

The confluence with the Cowlitz demands special attention because the two rivers meet nearly head-on with the Cispus sliding beneath the Cowlitz. Generally the easiest run is well to the right.

Scenery

The trip begins with a nice view of Tower Rock, but for the next 3.5 miles it is not very pretty, with many log jams on the gravel bars. The run between log time 55 minutes and 2 hours, 5 minutes, however, is exceptionally beautiful. Evergreen trees reach for the heavens straight up from the banks of the river, creating a cathedral-like effect. The clear water winds through a very rocky channel which alternates between gently flowing pools and fast, easy rapids. A number of cabins appear along the river in two stretches near the beginning of the trip, but below river mile 14 you see few signs of civilization. Several clearcuts become painfully evident once you emerge from the National Forest, but the more exciting whitewater takes your attention away from that "scenery."

Camping

Forest Service campgrounds are available at Tower Rock near river mile 15.7 and at Iron Creek near river mile 8. Check with the Randle Ranger Station (206) 497-7565 on when these campgrounds will be open; they may not open until well into May.

Rapids

The first part of the run has many gravel bars which make for fun little class 2 rapids, but the river channel really becomes interesting just above Iron Creek. Big boulders begin to appear in the river bed creating obstacles and rapids. *Let's Make a Deal* and *Roller Coaster* involve quick drops down chutes studded with huge boulders. Because of its relatively small water volume, the Cispus produces more technical rapids than big holes or waves, but some large holes and waves can form where the water gathers and goes over a good drop particularly at higher water levels.

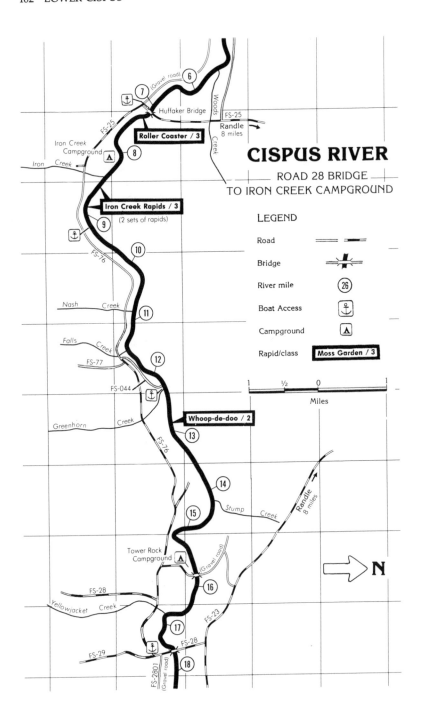

CISPUS RIVER

ROAD 28 BRIDGE
TO IRON CREEK CAMPGROUND

LEGEND

Road	
Bridge	
River mile	26
Boat Access	
Campground	
Rapid/class	Moss Garden / 3

Miles

Roller Coaster / 3

Iron Creek Rapids / 3
(2 sets of rapids)

Whoop-de-doo / 2

Huffaker Bridge

Iron Creek Campground

Tower Rock Campground

N

RIVER MILE	RIVER TIME	LEFT BANK	RAPIDS	RIGHT BANK	DESCRIPTION
	2:00	▲			—Iron Creek Campground left
					—Iron Creek left
	55		● 3		
			● 3		—**Iron Creek Rapids,** scout left along road
	50		● 2		—Nice small beach left
	45				
RM 10	40				
	35				
			● 2		
	30		● 2		—Beautiful, moss-covered bank left
			● 2		—Nash Creek left
	25		● 2		
			● 2		
	20				—Falls Creek left
			● 2		
	15		● 2		
	10	⚓	● 2		—Greenhorn Creek left
	5				
			● 2		—**Whoop-de-doo**
	1:00				
	55		● 2		
			● 2		
	50	▲			—Powerlines
	45	▲			—Stump Creek
			● 2		
	40	▲			
			● 2		
	35	▲			
RM 15	30		● 1		
	25		● 1		
		▲			—Tower Rock Campground left
	20				
	15				
	10				
	5				—Yellowjacket Creek left
	12:00	⚓			

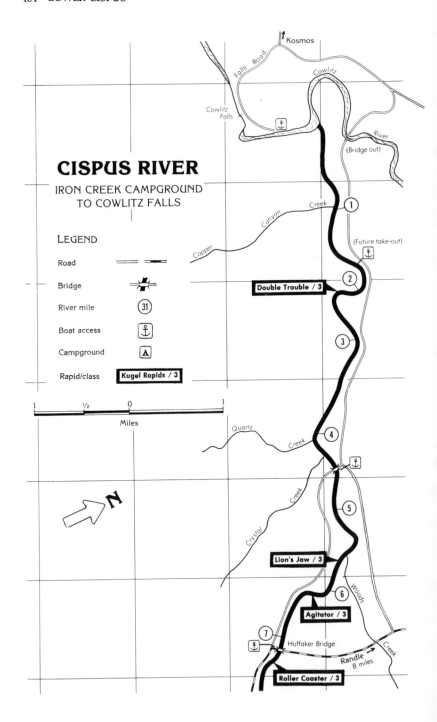

CISPUS RIVER

IRON CREEK CAMPGROUND
TO COWLITZ FALLS

LEGEND

Road

Bridge

River mile   (31)

Boat access

Campground

Rapid/class   Kugel Rapids / 3

Kosmos

Cowlitz

Falls Road

Cowlitz Falls

River
(Bridge out)

Canyon Creek

Copper

(1)

(Future take-out)

Double Trouble / 3   (2)

(3)

Quartz Creek

(4)

(5)

Crystal Creek

Lion's Jaw / 3

Woods

(6)

Agitator / 3

(7)

Huffaker Bridge

Randle
8 miles

Creek

Roller Coaster / 3

N

RIVER MILE	RIVER TIME	LEFT BANK	RAPIDS	RIGHT BANK	DESCRIPTION
	4:00				
	55				
	50				
	45		●3		—Boat ramp followed by white gauging station
RM 0	40		●2		—Headwall left
			●2 ●2		—Cowlitz River right
	35				
	30		●2 ●2		
	25		●2		
	20		●2 ●2		—Manicured garden right
					—Future boat-ramp
	15		●2		
			●3		—**Double Trouble,** run far right
	10		●2		—Shelter right bank
	5		●2		
	3:00		●2		
	55		●2		—Clearcut area left
			●2		—Quartz Creek left
	50				—Crystal Creek left
	45		●2		
RM 5	40				—Small beach left
			●2		
	35		●3		—Woods Creek
			●3		—**Lion's Jaw**
	30		●3		
			●3		—**Agitator,** run left, but stay off left bank
	25		●2		
			●2		
	20				—Huffaker Bridge
			●2		
	15		●3		—**Roller-coaster,** big waves at high water
			●3		—**Let's Make a Deal** can run either
	10		●2		side of island, more challenge left
			●3		
	5		●2		—Iron Creek Campground left
	2:00				

9

Entiat

Logged at - 10,200 cfs Peshastin gauge
Recommended water level - 5,500 to 11,000 cfs
Best time - May to mid-July
Rating - Advanced
Water level information - NOAA Tape (206) 526-8530
NOAA Information (206) 526-6087
River mile - 12.6 to 0.4; 12.2 miles
Time - 2 hours, 4 minutes; 6.1 mph
Elevation - 1345' to 720'; 51' per mile

Ardenvoir to Columbia River

The Entiat provides a fast ride on a small river in the eastern Washington sunshine. The Indian meaning of Entiat is "rapid water." There are no big rapids here, but nearly constant class 2 water, with occasional class 3 drops. Although signs of civilization are nearly always present, the scenery is generally pleasant, mainly farms and orchards. The Entiat is much less crowded and more intimate than the other east slope rivers which empty into the Columbia.

Getting There
The turn-off to the Entiat valley road is just south of the town of Entiat on US 97 about 16 miles north of Wenatchee.

Put-ins and Take-outs
About 0.2 mile up the Entiat River Road, you will see a portion of the old highway leaving the new road and going downriver closer to the river than the new road. This old highway provides access to the take-out. The take-out shown on the log as a light boat take-out is down a steep, short path to the river just downstream of a gate on the old highway. If the gate is closed, this is the best take-out to use.

If the gate is open, an easier take-out is farther down the old road and straight ahead for another 150 yards on the dirt road it becomes. Here you'll find an easy beach take-out. To reach it by river, go right around the final island and then come back up to the take-out on the slack water (backed up by Rocky Reach dam on the Columbia).

Finding a put-in on the Entiat is difficult because nearly all the land is privately owned. A small strip of Forest Service land provides access to the river 1.4 miles above a sign Wenatchee National Forest, Steliko Unit on your right (as you drive upriver). This sign is about 10 miles from the turn-off from US 97 on the Entiat valley road. The put-in is just upriver of a left bend in the river (right bend in the road as you drive upriver) and a turnout provides a parking area about 50 feet upstream on the side of the

Trees on the hillside and orchards on the valley floor
characterize the Entiat scenery.

At high water, the Entiat River has continuous whitewater.

road away from the river. Since the shoulder of the road next to the put-in is narrow, it is not a very good place to rig a raft.

There is more enjoyable class 2 to 3 boating for another 2 miles above this point (readily scouted from the road), but no public property on which to put in. So this is the uppermost put-in point unless you wish to knock on the door of a local resident and ask permission to put in.

Another potential small put-in is about 1.5 miles downriver, at the confluence with the Mad River, at log time 22 minutes. You can reach this spot by turning left off the Entiat valley road onto the Mad River Road about 9.5 miles from US 97. There is very little parking here, but it is easy access for kayaks.

Water Level

No gauge reports are available on the Entiat. The Entiat flows in a pattern very similar to the Wenatchee, however, so the gauge on the Wenatchee at Peshastin provides a good indication of water level on the Entiat. The Entiat is a good trip between 5,500 and 11,000 cfs on the Peshastin gauge. Below 5,500 it becomes quite rocky, while above 11,000 many of the rapids begin to wash-out and eddies become scarce.

Entiat
Peshastin Gauge
Recommend 5,500 to 11,000 cfs

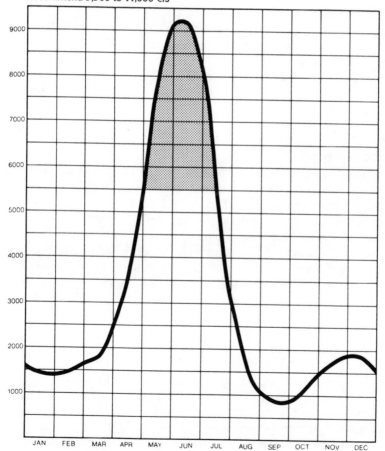

Special Hazards

The weir at log time one hour deserves special attention. While it is not a big drop and not difficult to run, it does present a perfect hydraulic which can hold a swimmer. At most water levels a tongue cuts through the hydraulic just to the right of center. You can scout here on the left bank. The old weir at log time 1 hour, 27 minutes has been breached on the right and presents no difficulties as long as it is run on the right.

At high water, finding an eddy can be difficult on the Entiat. The log was made at high water and I have indicated where eddies are to be found on the upper part of the run at such water levels for those who would like to take a break and regroup.

Scenery

Orchards, ranches and summer cabins line the Entiat. The mountain slopes in the distance are tree-covered at the put-in, sage-covered at the take-out. The water of the Entiat is clear when low and muddy-brown when high. It flows through a pleasant, narrow, dead-end valley, without many people or much junk on the banks.

Camping

There is a nice, small Forest Service campground at Pine Flat, about 4 miles up the Mad River road. It is not well signed; when the road turns to gravel and starts to climb up the ridge away from the river, take the unmarked turn-off down to the campground by the river. A short hike up the trail from the campground will bring you to the beautiful Mad River canyon. The Mad River provides the longest trail uninterrupted by roads along a river, outside of wilderness, on the east side of the Cascades. It is a prime candidate to become a Wild River in our national Wild & Scenic Rivers system.

There are numerous Forest Service campgrounds on up the Entiat itself. The first of these, Fox Creek, is about 28 miles from the Columbia and 14 miles above the put-in. The upper part of the river near these campgrounds provides a beautiful class 4 to 5 run for expert kayakers, but care should be taken to scout the dangerous and beautiful Box Canyon near Lake Creek Campground. Another scenic attraction is Entiat Falls on the main river, just below where the North Fork joins it some 34 miles above the

Constrictions in the river bed produce big waves.

Columbia. The upper Entiat and its North Fork have good fishing, beautiful scenery and would make a fine addition to our national Wild & Scenic Rivers system.

Rapids

The Entiat flows swiftly throughout the logged run; class 1 fast water quickly blends into class 2 waves and back again. The class 3 rapids are not much larger than the class 2s, but some large holes in them demand care. Particularly large waves occur in the section just above **Powerline Rapids.**

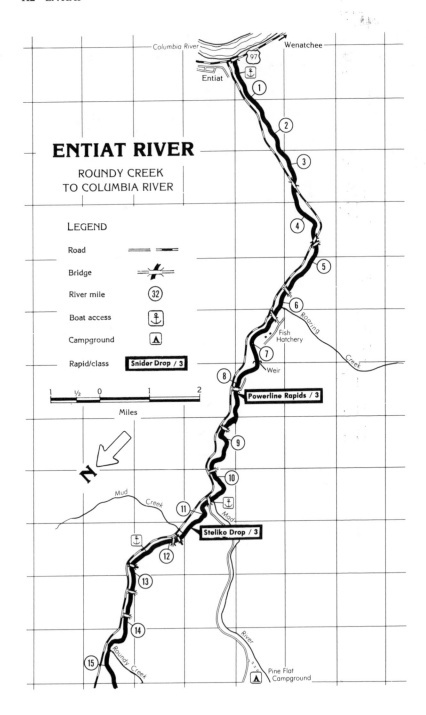

ENTIAT RIVER

ROUNDY CREEK
TO COLUMBIA RIVER

LEGEND

Road	
Bridge	
River mile	(32)
Boat access	
Campground	
Rapid/class	Snider Drop / 3

Columbia River

Wenatchee

97

Entiat

(1)
(2)
(3)
(4)
(5)
(6) Roaring Creek
Fish Hatchery
(7)
Weir
(8)
Powerline Rapids / 3
(9)
(10)
(11)
Mud Creek
Steliko Drop / 3
(12)
(13)
(14)
(15)
Roundy Creek

Mud River

Pine Flat Campground

½   0   1   2
Miles

N

RIVER MILE	RIVER TIME	LEFT BANK	RAPIDS	RIGHT BANK	DESCRIPTION
	2:00				—US 97 Bridge
	55				—Cable crossing
	50		●2		
	45		●3 ●2		
	40		●2		
	35		●2 ●2 ●2		
	30		●2 ●2 ●2		
	25				—Remains of old weir, run right —Two bridges
RM 5	20		●2		
	15		●2		
	10		●2 ●2		—Dilapidated footbridge
	5		●2 ●2 ●2 ●2		—Fish hatchery right
	1:00				—Weir, scout left, run tongue just right of center
	55		●2 ●2		
	50				—Eddies just below bridge on both sides
	45		●2 ●3 ●2		—Low cable followed by **Powerline Rapids**
	40		●3 ●2		—Eddy just above bridge right
	35		●2 ●2		—Footbridge followed by eddy right
RM 10	30		●2 ●2 ●3		
	25		●2 ●2		—Old bridge abutments both sides
	20		●2		‾Mad River right
	15		●3		—**Steliko Drop**
	10				—Bridge followed by rock and eddy left
	5		●2		
	12:00		●2 ●2 ●2		

10

Logged at - 2,300 cfs Buckley gauge
Recommended water level - 1,000 to 3,400 cfs
Best time - May to late July
Rating - Advanced
Water level information - NOAA Tape (206) 526-8530
NOAA Information (206) 526-6087
Army Corps (206) 764-3590
River mile - 51.5 to 38; 13.5 miles
Time - 2 hours, 3 minutes; 6.6 mph
Elevation - 1925' to 1330'; 44' per mile

West Fork Road to Bridge Camp

The White River is a hole-hog's delight. There are good holes to crash in rafts and to play in kayaks at all water levels. It's a quick trip from the Puget Sound area, and the glaciers on Mount Rainier provide water through the end of July. The White runs nearly clear in the spring and becomes milky in the summer, finally turning chocolate brown in late summer because of glacial silt.

Getting There
The White is paralleled by State Route 410 east of Enumclaw, some 35 miles southeast of Seattle. Enumclaw, named after a local mountain, means "home of the evil spirits."

Put-ins and Take-outs
To reach the take-out, head out of Enumclaw on State Route 410 toward Cayuse and Chinook passes. About three miles out of town, you'll pass the turn-off to Mud Mountain Dam on the White below the logged run. Going 5.3 miles farther up the road you'll pass mile marker 35. The turn-off to Bridge Camp is on an unmarked dirt road 0.35 miles beyond mile marker 35.

Splashing through the milky water of the White River

You'll pass immediately through a gate (closed by the Weyerhaeuser Company in times of high fire danger) and wind down a
switchback to a Weyerhaeuser road paralleling State Route 410.
Cross this road and the bridge immediately beyond it and turn
right into the unimproved Bridge Camp.

About three miles farther upriver the Weyerhaeuser road
crosses the river on a concrete bridge visible from the highway.
This bridge is on the log at 1 hour, 29 minutes and provides an alternate, though steep, put-in or take-out.

The town of Greenwater is about five miles farther upriver. Two
miles beyond the Greenwater General Store is a log overpass.
Turning right just before the overpass, you'll reach another alternate put-in or take-out point at a bridge over the river at log time
20 minutes.

The put-in on the West Fork White River Road is on Forest Service 74 road. The turn-off to the 74 road is 0.4 mile beyond

milepost 46 which is 3.2 miles beyond the Greenwater General Store.

Water Level

The Army Corps (which operates the Mud Mountain Dam) maintains a gauge on the river, which measures flow in the area of the dam. It is called the White River above Buckley. The White is a good run for rafts and kayaks from 1,000 to 3,400 cfs. Above 3,400, there are very few eddies, the water is very swift and rescue is difficult. Below 1,000, several gravel bars are exposed making it difficult for rafts, but kayakers who don't mind scraping a bit will find good holes to play in down to 700 cfs.

Bridges across the river are the major landmarks.

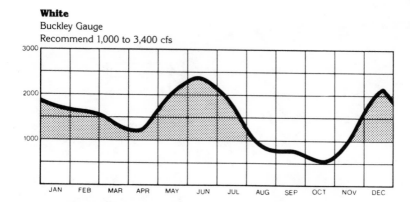

White
Buckley Gauge
Recommend 1,000 to 3,400 cfs

Special Hazards

The Osceola Mudflow, one of the largest mudflows in the world, filled the valley of the White 150 years ago. As a result, the valley is full of loose soil and rocks; bedrock is buried hundreds of feet below. The soft banks are constantly being eroded and the river channel frequently shifts, dropping many trees into the river and creating frequent log jams. Stay alert!

Scenery

Nice views of Mt. Rainier appear at several points along the river, but the immediate river shore is not very pretty. Although there are not many man-made structures for most of the trip, many of the surrounding banks have been recently clearcut and frequent log jams occur on the gravel bars.

Camping

Campsites are available at the State's Federation Forest Campground a little below Greenwater and at the Forest Service's Dalles Campground about 4 miles above the put-in.

Rapids

The White provides lots of waves and easily crashable holes which make for a fun trip. **Cyclone Drop** begins a series of rapids and an exciting end to the run. These are rocky ledge drops, with few obstacles. The only rapid with many exposed boulders is at log time 1 hour, 33 minutes.

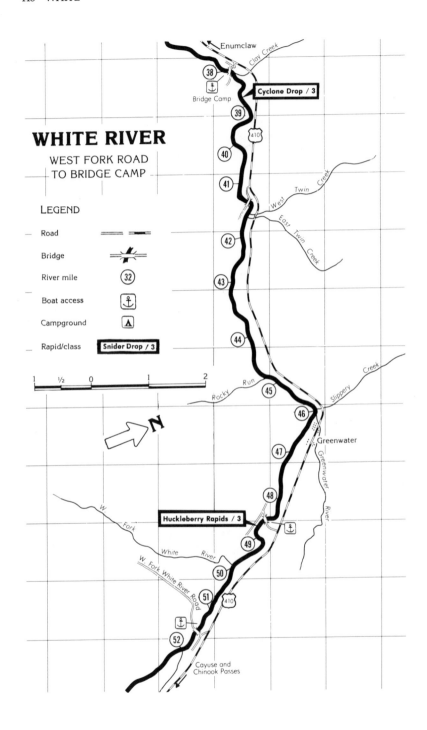

WHITE RIVER

WEST FORK ROAD TO BRIDGE CAMP

LEGEND

Road	
Bridge	
River mile	32
Boat access	
Campground	
Rapid/class	Snider Drop / 3

Enumclaw

Clay Creek

38

Bridge Camp

Cyclone Drop / 3

39

410

40

41

West Twin Creek

East Twin Creek

42

43

44

Rocky Run

Slippery Creek

45

46

Greenwater

47

Greenwater River

48

Huckleberry Rapids / 3

49

W. Fork

White River

W. Fork White River Road

50

51

410

52

Cayuse and Chinook Passes

N

RIVER MILE	RIVER TIME	LEFT BANK	RAPIDS	RIGHT BANK	DESCRIPTION
		⚓			—Bridge Camp left
	2:00		●3 ●2		
			●3		
	55		●3		
			❘ ●3		—**Cyclone Drop**
	50		●2 ●2		
	45				
			●3		
RM 40	40		❘ ☼		—Bad log jam
					—Road next to right bank
	35		●2		
			●3		
	30		●2		
			●2		—East and West Twin Creeks
	25				
					—Powerlines
	20				
			●2		
	15		●2		
			❘		
	10				
			●2		
	5		●2		
			❘		
	1:00				
			●3		
RM 45	55		●2		—Rocky Run left
			●2		
	50		●2		
			●2❘		
	45		●2		—Slippery Creek right
			●2		—Greenwater River right
	40		●2		—Cabin with Greenwater sign right
			●2		
	35				
			●2		
	30		●2		
			●2		
	25		●2		
			❘●3	⚓	
	20				
			●3		—**Huckleberry Rapids**
	15		●2		
			●3	❙	—Headwall right
RM 50	10		❘●2		—West Fork left
	5		●2 ●2		
		⚓	●2		
	12:00				—West Fork Road Bridge

11

Lower Spokane

Logged at - 12,000 cfs Spokane gauge
Recommended water level - 4,000 to 19,000 cfs
Best time - April to June
Rating - Advanced
Water level information - NOAA Tape (206) 526-8530
NOAA Information (206) 526-6087
Washington Water Power (509) 489-0500 (Ext. 2141)
River mile - 69.8 to 63.5; 6.3 miles
Time - 1 hour, 13 minutes; 4.8 mph
Elevation - 1675' to 1605'; 11' per mile

Fort Wright Bridge to Seven Mile Bridge

In spite of the fact that this run starts right within the city of Spokane, the heavily forested, steep river valley is quite pretty. There are numerous signs of civilization, including a sewage plant, but the broad river and spectacular rock formations make you forget that this trip is so near to town. The trip is largely class 1 and 2, but there are two serious class 3 rapids. Even though there are not many difficult rapids, the volume of water in the river creates strong hydraulics and the river demands respect.

Getting There

From I-90, take the Maple Toll Bridge exit 280 and follow the signs to the Maple Toll Bridge (25 cents for cars to cross). Continue north on Maple 1.3 miles past the toll bridge and turn left on Northwest Boulevard. Go approximately 0.7 mile on Northwest Boulevard and make another left at a stop light on T. J. Meenach

Looking back upriver at Bowl & Pitcher

Drive. A short distance down the drive, you will reach the Fort Wright Bridge.

Put-ins and Take-outs

Take a right just before the Fort Wright Bridge and turn into the turn-out area to park. From here you can carry your boat down to the water. Excessive use of the area by four-wheel drive vehicles has torn up the hillside so much that two-wheel drive vehicles can rarely negotiate it.

To reach an easier put-in, drive downriver on Downriver Drive approximately 1 mile from the Fort Wright Bridge to where a dirt road turns off the main road downriver. The main road cuts across a bend in the river while the dirt road follows the river bank in front of a nursing home. The dirt road continues downriver and reconnects with Downriver Drive about 0.3 mile below where it left the Drive.

To reach the take-out, continue downstream on Downriver Drive, past the entrance to Riverside State Park. About 2 miles below the entrance to the park, you'll pass under a set of powerlines; 0.5 mile below that is the take-out. There is a small, paved turnout road on the river side of the main road. Running upriver from this turnout is an unused dirt road which provides a convenient path to the water.

Note that park regulations prohibit putting in or taking out in the main part of Riverside State Park where the camping and picnicking facilities are near **Bowl & Pitcher.** The state doesn't want

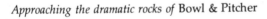

Approaching the dramatic rocks of Bowl & Pitcher

to give ideas to anyone using these public facilities, who might try running the river with inadequate equipment and no understanding of the potentially dangerous hydraulics in a large river. People are killed on this stretch of the Spokane nearly every year simply because it is accessible to so many people who have no idea what dangers they face.

Water Level

The Lower Spokane provides an exciting run from 4,000 to 19,000 cfs on the Spokane gauge. Below 4,000 cfs the run is a real bottom scraper.

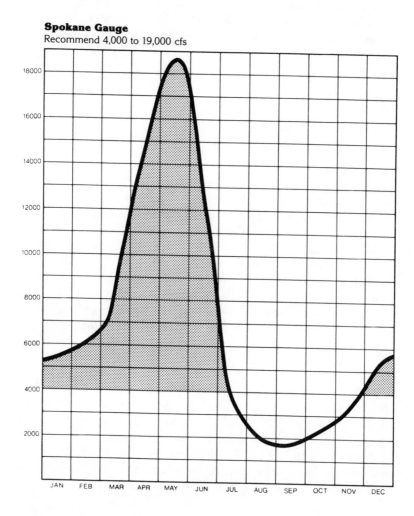

Spokane Gauge
Recommend 4,000 to 19,000 cfs

Special Hazards

The great volume of water in the Lower Spokane can make for very powerful hydraulics. You shouldn't run the river above 19,000 cfs unless you are already familiar with its currents and power from making runs at lower water levels.

Scenery

The steep sides of the river valley, covered with a pretty, semi-open pine forest, make the trip very pleasant. Not many buildings are visible, but you get several reminders of civilization, such as the sewage treatment plant. The spectacular volcanic rock outcroppings make **Bowl & Pitcher** one of the most interesting class 3 rapids in the state. The water surges through several passages between huge pillars of volcanic rock.

Camping

There are many campsites available in Riverside State Park near **Bowl & Pitcher.** A fee is charged.

Rapids

The big rapids of the trip are **Bowl & Pitcher** and **Devil's Toenail.** Because of the large volume of water in the Spokane, these rapids can provide some powerful hydraulics. The best way to scout them is on the shuttle.

To take a look at **Bowl & Pitcher,** turn in the main entrance to Riverside State Park, take the third spur road to the right, and park in the parking area. From here you can see the footbridge which crosses the river. Walk out on the footbridge to scout the rapid. It begins above the footbridge and continues another 100 yards below it through the dramatic rock formations which give **Bowl & Pitcher** its name. There are several good play waves right below the footbridge and kayakers usually eddy out on the right just below the bridge to try their luck on the waves.

To scout the **Devil's Toenail,** continue downriver 0.9 mile from the entrance of the park to **Bowl & Pitcher** (or 1.6 mile above the take-out, going the other direction) and park on the paved turnout on the outside of a bend along the river. Scramble down the slope to the river's edge for a look. The run is near the right bank where you are standing. Some large rocks here on the right bank provide a good place to take pictures.

Sun and whitewater just below the capital of the Inland Empire

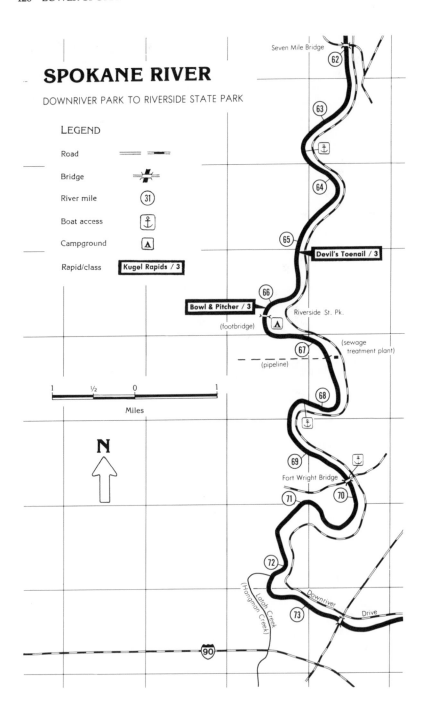

SPOKANE RIVER

DOWNRIVER PARK TO RIVERSIDE STATE PARK

LEGEND

Road

Bridge

River mile   (31)

Boat access

Campground   A

Rapid/class   **Kugel Rapids / 3**

Seven Mile Bridge   (62)

(63)

(64)

(65)

Devil's Toenail / 3

(66)

Bowl & Pitcher / 3

(footbridge)   Riverside St. Pk.

A

(67)   (sewage treatment plant)

(pipeline)

(68)

1   ½   0   1

Miles

N

(69)

Fort Wright Bridge

(71)   (70)

(72)

Downriver

(Hangman Creek)

Latah Creek

(73)   Drive

90

RIVER MILE	RIVER TIME	LEFT BANK	RAPIDS	RIGHT BANK	DESCRIPTION
	2:00				
	55				
	50				
	45				
	40				
	35				
	30				
	25				
	20				
	15			⚓	
	10		●2		—Powerlines cross —Beach left
	5			⬆	—Gun club right
RM 65	1:00				
	55		●3		—**Devil's Toenail** (Dragon's Teeth), run right
	50		●2		—Powerlines
	45		●3		—**Bowl & Pitcher,** enter on tongue right of center
	40		●2	◢△	—Riverside State Park right
	35				—Pipeline & footbridge signed Warning—Dangerous Rapids
	30			⬆	—Sewage Treatment Plant
				〰	—Outlet from sewage treatment plant
	25				
	20			⚓	
	15			⬆	—Nursing home right
	10	⬆			—White building left
	5				
			▮	◢	—Small island with trees, run either side
	12:00				—Fort Wright Bridge

12

Chiwawa

Logged at - 7,000 cfs Peshastin gauge
Recommended water level - 5,000 to 10,000 cfs
Best time - May to mid-July
Rating - Advanced
Water level information - NOAA Tape (206) 526-8530
NOAA Information (206) 526-6087
River mile - 12.8 to Wenatchee mile 46.5; 14.7 miles
Time - 2 hours, 53 minutes; 5.1 mph
Elevation - 2380' to 1810'; 39' per mile

Huckleberry Ford to Plain

The Chiwawa provides a fast and exciting ride through largely untouched eastern Washington forest. The rapids are nearly constant in the three gorge stretches and you only have time to catch your breath in the sections between. This is the closest river trip to the Puget Sound area where you can enjoy beautiful scenery in the sunny skies of eastern Washington.

Getting There

State Route 207 turns off US 2 at Coles Corner about 21 miles east of Stevens Pass or 16 miles west of Leavenworth. If you go five miles north on 207, you'll come to its intersection with State Route 209. A right turn on 209 will take you, in about five miles, to the take-out at the bridge over the Wenatchee. Traveling straight ahead on 207 will take you to the put-in.

Put-ins and Take-outs

The take-out is just north of the bridge over the Wenatchee on the east side of the river near the town of Plain. An alternative take-out for those who wish to avoid the quieter water at the end of the trip (or a put-in for those seeking a less exciting trip) is at the bridge over the Chiwawa at about river mile 2. It can be reached by continuing north from the 207-209 intersection and bearing right after crossing the Wenatchee in the direction of signs pointing to Fish Lake and the Chiwawa river Road. If you continue straight ahead (and not up the Chiwawa road) for a little more than four miles, you'll reach the bridge.

To reach the put-in, follow State Route 207 across the Wenatchee River, then turn right. About 1.5 miles farther, turn

Hotdogging the Chiwawa

left on the road toward Chiwawa River and Trinity. This road will take you by Fish Lake and then cross the Chiwawa on the bridge which is at log time 1 hour, ten minutes. This could serve as either a put-in or take-out for shorter runs.

To reach the upper put-in, turn left on the Chiwawa River road (toward Trinity) about 0.5 mile after crossing the bridge. Approximately 6 miles up this road, Huckleberry Ford is reached by turning left and going 0.2 mile onto an unmarked dirt road. This turn-off is 0.1 mile beyond a sign for Upper Grouse Creek Campground.

Huckleberry Ford could be used as a take-out point for those who would like to go for a river canoeing trip. The river is nearly flat from Schaefer Creek Campground to here, about twelve miles. There are many log jams in the river, though, requiring numerous portages. Canoeing skill is also needed to avoid the many rocks that stud the slow moving current. Only expert whitewater canoeists should attempt the river below Huckleberry Ford in a canoe; the nearly continuous whitewater found in many stretches would swamp any but the most perfectly handled canoes.

Water Level

There is no gauge operating on the Chiwawa River, but historical water records reveal that the Chiwawa normally contributes about 20% of the water in the Wenatchee River at Peshastin. The Chiwawa should provide you with an exciting first run at levels between 5,000 and 10,000 cfs on the Peshastin gauge. I wouldn't recommend the river above 10,000 cfs until you are familiar with it, since its steep slope makes for nearly continuous whitewater at higher levels.

Special Hazards

The Chiwawa is a fast run but presents no great hazards. There is a low cable across the river at log time 22 minutes (river mile 11) which requires moving far right or left at high water. Care should also be taken in determining which side of an island you choose to go around as some passages are completely blocked by logs. The islands are small enough, however, that the jams can always be seen before you commit yourself.

The log jams change from year to year and you must always remain alert to the possibility that the river could be completely blocked.

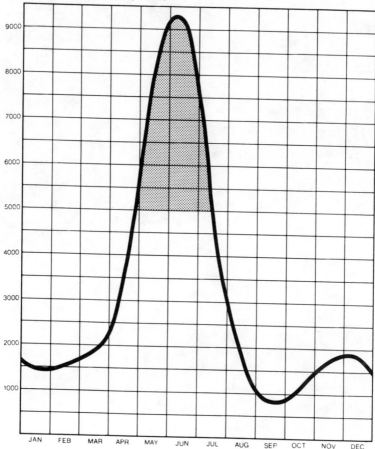

Chiwawa
Peshastin Gauge
Recommend 5,000 to 10,000 cfs

Scenery

The Chiwawa will treat you to nearly unspoiled eastern Washington forested river banks. The river channel is fairly narrow with few islands. The largely fir forest is interspersed with numerous cedars in the lower end around Goose Creek Gorge. There are a few gravel beaches for nice lunch stops. Watch for the beaches just around the inside of river bends; if you aren't ready to pull in before you see them, you'll never make it.

The banks of the Chiwawa are heavily forested.

The Forest Service has recommended that the Chiwawa be added to the National Wild & Scenic River System. If you enjoy boating the Chiwawa, write your Congressman and help preserve this beautiful river for us all to enjoy.

Camping

There are numerous Forest Service campgrounds around the Chiwawa. Meadow Creek and Goose Creek campgrounds along the river are shown on the map. It would be easy to even pull your boat up at Big Meadow Creek campground if you were inclined to stop on your way down the river and continue the next day. Grouse Creek campground is a Group Reservation Site and you must obtain permission from the Forest Service before camping there. Check with the Lake Wenatchee Ranger Station at (509) 763-3103 or 763-3211. In addition, Lake Wenatchee State Park has campsites available at the east end of the lake.

Rapids

The rapids on this trip come in distinct sets which I have labeled as gorges even though they don't have the sort of narrow defiles often associated with gorges. Each gorge is named after the creek which comes into the river at its beginning. Each gorge presents you with nearly continuous whitewater that demands constant attention until you are hurled out of it by the swift current.

The water does not slow down very much even in the sections between the gorges, but the lack of obstacles and little waves there give you a chance to relax and bail. Eddies are few and landing a raft requires that you anticipate where an eddy is likely to be found and start pulling for it even before you see whether it is there or not.

The whitewater in Gate Creek and Big Meadow Creek gorges mostly consists of waves with few obstacles. The drops in Goose Creek Gorge present you with more obstacles and are more interesting challenges. The bulk of the whitewater is over after Goose Creek Gorge, but you still have a pleasant float to the bridge near Plain. The easier whitewater of the lower portion of the run provides good training for those graduating from beginning to intermediate boaters. The big difference between the size of the Chiwawa and the Wenatchee is dramatically revealed when you drift out of the narrow Chiwawa onto the broad Wenatchee.

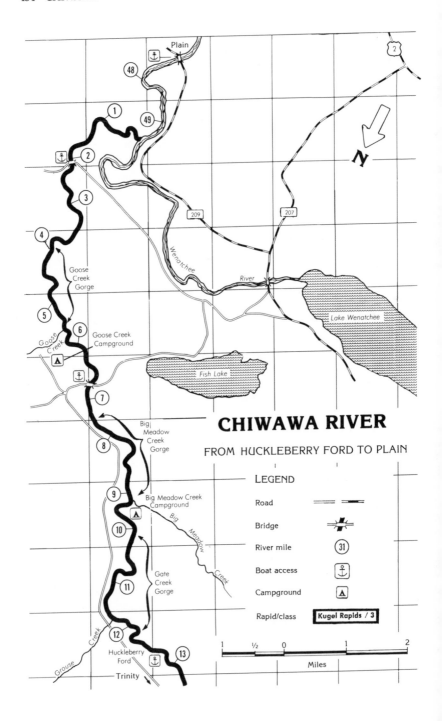

Plain

48

1

49

2

3

4

Goose
Creek
Gorge

5

6   Goose Creek
Campground

7

8   Big
Meadow
Creek
Gorge

9   Big Meadow Creek
Campground

10   Big

11   Gate
Creek
Gorge

12

13

Huckleberry
Ford

Trinity

Grouse Creek

Goose Creek

Big Meadow Creek

Wenatchee River

Lake Wenatchee

Fish Lake

209

207

2

N

CHIWAWA RIVER

FROM HUCKLEBERRY FORD TO PLAIN

LEGEND

Road	
Bridge	
River mile	31
Boat access	
Campground	A
Rapid/class	Kugel Rapids / 3

1   ½   0   1   2

Miles

RIVER MILE	RIVER TIME	LEFT BANK	RAPIDS	RIGHT BANK	DESCRIPTION
	2:00				
	55		●2 ●2		—Good playspot, open bluff right
	50				
	45	■	●2 ●2		—Irrigation diversion gate left
	40	△	●2 ☆ ●2		—Log jam right
	35	△	●3 * ●2 ●3 ●3		—Boulders right / —Big waves
RM 5	30		●2		
	25		●3 ●2 ●2		—Big hole center, run right or left
	20	∼∼∼	●2	△	—Goose Creek left
	15	△	●2		
	10	△ △	❙ ■	△	—Bare dirt cliffs right / —Chiwawa River Bridge / Potential campsites and boat access both sides
	5				
	1:00		●2 ●2 ●2 ●2		—Good playspot at ledge
	55				
	50		●2 ●2 ●2		—Logs block right channel
	45		●2 ●2 ●2	∼∼∼	—Big Meadow Creek right
	40		●2	△	—Big Meadow Creek Campground
RM 10	35				
	30	△	●2 ●2 ●2 ●3 ●3		—Campsite just beyond sharp left bend
	25		●2 ●3 ●2		—Nice waves
	20	◆—◆—◆	●2		—Low cable crossing, go far right or left
	15		●2 ●3 ●2 ●2		—Thread-the-Needle, run center or right
	10	∼∼∼ △	●2 ●2		—Logs block left channel / —Grouse Creek left
	5	∼∼∼ ■	●2 ●2		—Good eddies both sides / —Gate Creek left
	12:00	⚓			—Huckleberry Ford

Above: Nose-plugs come in handy when the action gets heavy. Below: There are few eddies for all those playspots; catch them on your way down.

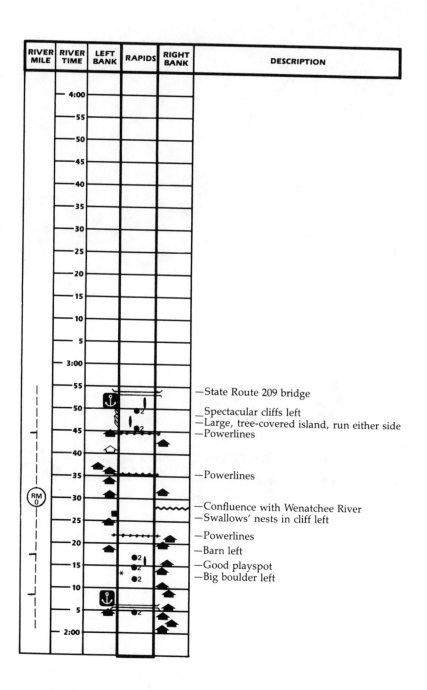

RIVER MILE	RIVER TIME	LEFT BANK	RAPIDS	RIGHT BANK	DESCRIPTION
	4:00				
	55				
	50				
	45				
	40				
	35				
	30				
	25				
	20				
	15				
	10				
	5				
	3:00				
	55				—State Route 209 bridge
	50				_Spectacular cliffs left
	45				—Large, tree-covered island, run either side —Powerlines
	40				
	35				—Powerlines
RM 0	30				
	25				—Confluence with Wenatchee River —Swallows' nests in cliff left
	20				—Powerlines
	15				—Barn left —Good playspot —Big boulder left
	10				
	5				
	2:00				

Getting your money's worth out of a hole

13

Snoqualmie, North Fork

Logged at - 1,050 cfs North Fork gauge
Recommended water level - 600 to 1,600 cfs
Best time - late April through June
Rating - Advanced
Water level information - NOAA Tape (206) 526-8530
NOAA Information (206) 526-6087
King County (206) 225-2531
River mile - 11.7 to 5.4; 6.3 miles
Time - 1 hour, 30 minutes; 4.2 mph
Elevation - 1270' to 1020'; 40' per mile

Deep Creek to Swinging Bridge

The North Fork of the Snoqualmie has one of the most interesting river channels to be found in Washington. Its narrow stream bed—large boulders in the channel and wide variety of pools, drops, ledges, chutes, rock gardens and gravel bars—provides the greatest diversity of challenges on any six mile stretch of river in the state.

Since it has been one of the favorite runs of the Washington Kayak Club and the University of Washington Canoe Club for many years, it is not really a lesser known run as suggested in this book's subtitle, but it is not well known outside of western Washington. It is currently threatened with destruction by a dam planned by the City of Bellevue for an ill-considered water supply

Kayakers go into orbit over the North Fork.

project. The dam would be located at the bridge at log time 1 hour, 8 minutes. It would be 240 feet high and flood the river back to the mouth of Deep Creek, less than 0.5 mile below the put-in. If you would like to help stop this avoidable destruction, contact Friends of Whitewater, mentioned in the Preface.

This trip is difficult for rafts. It can be run in a raft (that's how I made the log in the book), but there are several obstacles to rafting the river: (1) Rafts need 800 cfs to run the river and it only has that much flow for a few unpredictable weeks during the year, (2) the trip is only 1 hour, 30 minutes long and the shuttle takes nearly 1 hour to drive round-trip on the dirt roads (shortness is not a problem for kayakers due to the number of great playspots), (3) because the North Fork has such small water volume, there is a much greater chance of the channel being completely blocked by fallen trees than on other rivers in this book, and (4) the put-in and take-out are quite difficult—50-yard carries through the woods.

Getting There

Take exit 31 from I-90 and go west on State Route 202 about 0.5 mile into the town of North Bend. Turn right on North Bend Way (the main street in town). In about one block turn left immediately after Loveland Chevrolet and Olds on Ballarat Ave. North. Ballarat turns and twists; stay on it. After 0.5 mile it ceases to be called Ballarat and becomes 108th Street, then NE 12th St., then 428th St. NE.

Stay on the main road and just over 2 miles outside of downtown North Bend, cross a new concrete bridge over the Middle Fork of the Snoqualmie. Shortly afterwards, the route crosses an older bridge over the North Fork and becomes North Fork Road. One and one-half miles after crossing the North Fork, the road divides. There are Dead End signs at both forks. Take the left fork which has signs saying Dead End and For 24 Miles.

Put-ins and Take-outs

About 0.5 mile up the road, the pavement ends. Check your odometer because the turn-off to the take-out is one mile from here on an unmarked dirt road. It turns off to the right as you head up hill; the main road bears to the left.

To get to the take-out follow the unmarked dirt road through clearcuts about 0.5 mile to a Y and bear left. At 0.8 mile beyond the Y, stay to the right. About 0.1 mile farther, roads branch off to

There are no signs of civilization along the banks.

both the right and the left. Continue straight ahead on the now very narrow road into the woods. In about 0.1 mile you will reach a clearing which is usually the end of the road for two-wheel drive vehicles. Four-wheel drive vehicles can continue another 50 yards down to the right to a spot just above the river.

The easiest take-out is reached at the end of a 50 yard trail leaving the end of the road and heading downriver through the woods. You should tie a flag on a tree at the take-out or you will have great difficulty recognizing it from the river. Do *not* go beyond the take-out. If you do, you'll encounter class 6 water leading to a waterfall—not fun.

To get to the put-in, return to the main road and continue up about 2.5 miles to an intersection. To the right is a gated turn-off with a sign saying Snoqualmie Tree Farm. (This road would take you to the bridge over the river at log time 1 hour, 5 minutes. Due to the steep banks, this is not an easy put-in or take-out.) Another

5.5 miles farther, you'll cross a bridge over Deep Creek (not signed). At 0.6 mile later, park along the main road to scramble down the bank to the river (this is near where a road into an old campground has been blocked by a ditch and felled trees). Do not boat above the put-in. Between Wagner Bridge (just upstream 0.3 mile) and the put-in is class 6 water.

Water Level

From 600 to 1,600 cfs on the North Fork gauge the North Fork is a great run for kayaks. Above 1,600 many of the drops begin to wash out. Rafts need a minimum of 800 cfs to avoid scraping on gravel bars.

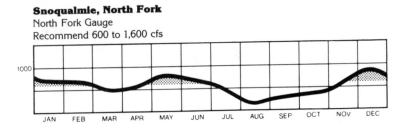

Snoqualmie, North Fork
North Fork Gauge
Recommend 600 to 1,600 cfs

Special Hazards

Because of the small water volume of this river, it is quite easy for trees to fall all the way across the channel; watch out for sweepers.

Scenery

Although the surrounding forest has been heavily clearcut, the scenery from the river is superb. A strip of trees along the river screens out most evidence of logging, and other than one bridge and a couple of cables, there are no signs of civilization. A fascinating feature of the North Fork is the number of very large boulders in the middle of the channel. They highlight the scenery and provide interesting obstacles. There are also beautiful rock walls and nice small beaches.

Camping

Wagner Bridge campground, operated by the State Department of Natural Resources, is just across Wagner Bridge about 0.5 mile upstream from the put-in. All of the land in this area belongs to the Weyerhaeuser Company which has no objection to people camping as long as they stay out of the way of logging operations.

Rapids

Deep Creek Drop provides a good place to play and a warm up for what's ahead. It sweeps over a gravel bar and then around a right bend to a good drop at the end. The most difficult rapids are the series of class 3 drops at log time 21 to 27 minutes and a second series near the end at log time 1 hour, 18 to 27 minutes. Both series of rapids involve four or five drops coming so close together that they become one long rapid approaching class 4 in difficulty because of its length. About two-thirds of the way through the first series, you'll encounter an exciting 3 foot ledge drop. The biggest hydraulics of the trip are found in the rapid at log time 53 minutes and in **Hancock** where passage is found between the right bank and a large boulder near the right shore.

Play until you drop.

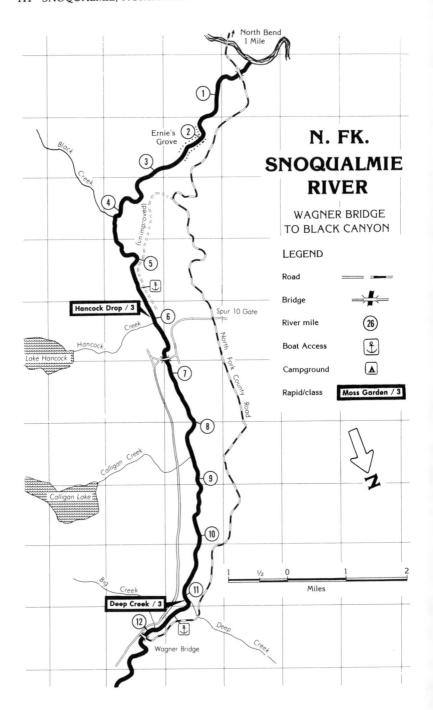

North Bend
1 Mile

N. FK.
SNOQUALMIE
RIVER

WAGNER BRIDGE
TO BLACK CANYON

LEGEND

Road

Bridge

River mile   (26)

Boat Access

Campground

Rapid/class   **Moss Garden / 3**

N

Ernie's
Grove

Black Creek

Hancock Drop / 3

Creek

Spur 10 Gate

Hancock

Lake Hancock

North Fork County Road

Calligan Creek

Calligan Lake

Big Creek

Deep Creek / 3

Deep Creek

Wagner Bridge

1   ½   0   1   2
Miles

RIVER MILE	RIVER TIME	LEFT BANK	RAPIDS	RIGHT BANK	DESCRIPTION
	2:00				
	55				
	50				
	45				
	40				
	35				
	30			⚓	
	25		•2 •3 I •3		
	20		•3 •2 •3		
	15	∿∿	•2		—**Hancock Drop,** run right, good playspot —Hancock Creek left
	10		I		—Spur 10 Bridge
	5	∿∿	•2 •2		
	1:00				
	55		•2		
	50		•3 •2 •2		—Good playspot
	45	∿∿			—Calligan Creek left
	40	■	•2 •2 •3	■	—Beach left —Large rock-sided "island" with trees on top right
	35	■	•?		—Old gauge and cable crossing
	30	∿∿	•2 •2 •2 •3	■	—Beach right —Eddy right
	25		•3 •3 •3		
	20		•2		
	15		•3		
	10		•3 •2	■	—**Deep Creek Drop** —Large rock right
	5		•2 •2 •2		
	12:00		•2		

RM 10

14

Kalama

Logged at - 1,850 cfs on Kalama gauge
Recommended water level - 1,100 to 3,200 cfs
Best time - April to early May
Rating - Advanced
Water level information - NOAA Tape (206) 526-8530
NOAA Information (206) 526-6087
River mile - 20.4 to 10.9; 9.5 miles
Time - 2 hours, 14 minutes; 4.2 mph
Elevation - 450' to 170'; 29' per mile

Pigeon Springs to Lower Kalama Falls

The Kalama is my favorite early season run. It combines beautiful scenery with fun whitewater. Having just a couple of challenging drops, it gets the season off to a good start on a small, intimate river. The Indian meaning of Kalama is "fair maiden." Others praise the river as well. Fly fishermen revere the upper part of the river as the "holy water" and salmon and steelhead fishermen flock to the river below the falls for the perfect fishing trip.

Getting There
The Kalama is about 30 miles north of Portland on I-5. Turn off at the Kalama River Road exit and drive east some nine beautiful miles to the Washington State Salmon Hatchery, the take-out.

Put-ins and Take-outs
The take-out at the salmon hatchery is just beyond the parking lot and to the left, behind some houses. It is an excellent take-out, with a broad, fairly level, gravel beach. Leave your vehicles in the parking lot and take them down to the bank only for loading.

About one-half mile above the hatchery, the road divides. The upper road is in better condition and will get you to the upper put-in.

A narrow, rock-walled gorge highlights the Kalama scenery.

The upper put-in is just above a concrete bridge over the river next to a very broad dirt turn-out. The surrounding area has been completely logged. The put-in is steep and rugged, but it's the only one on this section of the river.

To reach the intermediate access point, take the lower road 0.5 mile above the hatchery. About 1.8 miles above the fork in the road, you will pass a suspension bridge (designed for cars, but I wouldn't want to test it) over the river. About 0.9 mile beyond the suspension bridge is a steep short path to an eddy through a stand of evergreens. It is a good place to take out for those who

Above: There's quite a jolt at the bottom of Whats That? Falls.
Below: Winter floods deposit logs high on the rocks.

want to avoid the flatwater and a good place to put in for those seeking a class 1 canoe trip.

Water Level

Although the Kalama drains the west side of Mt. Saint Helens, most of its drainage is under 3,000 feet in elevation so it does not have enough snow run-off to provide good water levels in late spring or summer. Some recent rain is usually necessary to have enough water for boating, and the river is usually only at runnable levels in the late fall, winter and early spring.

I recommend 1,100 cfs minimum for a good trip, though kayaks could probably sneak down the river on 800 cfs. Because the gauge is quite a way farther downriver, it probably shows a third again as much water as is in the logged run.

Kalama
Kalama Gauge
Recommend 1,100 to 3,200 cfs

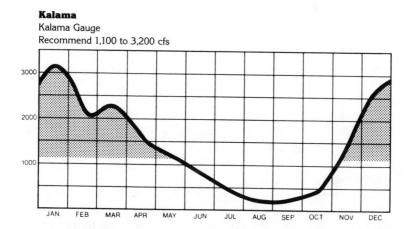

Special Hazards

Avoid **Lower Kalama Falls.** The principal drop is about 15 feet and has been subjected to man-made "improvements" which create a perfect hydraulic. At most water levels a boater would be lucky to survive a trip over the falls. The falls are only about 500 feet below the take-out at the salmon hatchery, so don't miss it! The hatchery take-out is easy to spot, but don't day-dream.

Scenery

There is near rain-forest beauty on this small river. Much of the banks are lined with thick forest and moss-covered rock outcrop-

Now, was it right or left of the gray rock?

pings. A couple hundred yards of the river, at log time 58 minutes, flow through solid rock walls like a miniature Mule Creek Canyon. The creek at log time 1 hour, 4 minutes enters the river over a series of beautiful little falls. The lower portion of the run provides some of the most unspoiled scenery of the trip, but almost no whitewater.

Camping

A campsite is not easy to come by near the Kalama. The nearest public campground is Speelyai, operated by Pacific Power and Light at the lower end of Lake Merwin on the Lewis River. To get there, travel south some 10 miles on I-5 to Woodland and take State Route 503 east toward Cougar about 12 miles.

Rapids

Most of the rapids on the Kalama are very enjoyable class 2s which have an abundance of good playspots. The two rapids which may deserve a scout are **What's That? Falls** and **Leader Rapids.** You may also wish to take a look at **Summers Creek Drop,** right under the concrete Summers Creek bridge, on the drive to the put-in. It is easily run right down the middle, however.

What's That? Falls acquired its name from our reaction to seeing a horizon line and boiling whitewater below, when we

Trying to follow the leader through Leader

first ran the river based on some sketchy reports. It's quite a straightforward drop, but much more easily run if you scout the correct line for the tongue rather than try to pick it out as you bear down on it. You should land just around a left bend in the river, above a short class 2 rapid. Once you enter the class 2, you're committed to **What's That? Falls.**

Leader Rapids is only marginally class 4 at most of the recommended water levels, but definitely requires a scout on the right bank before running it. None of the moves required is very difficult, but there are so many boulders staggered down the drop that it is essential to have a route planned in advance. Above 1,600 cfs **Leader Rapids** can be run either on the right or on the left. Below 1,600 cfs, rocks exposed on the right suggest the left-hand route.

Kayakers may wish to consider running a very exciting, but short, part of the river below the section logged and below the Lower Kalama Falls. Because the road is some distance above the river at this point, a put-in requires a steep carry down some 120 vertical feet of rough hillside to the river. Make sure that you put in *below* **Lower Kalama Falls!** You'll be rewarded with a 2.5 mile canyon run having two class 4 and a half dozen class 3 rapids before the road returns to the river bank at Indian Creek. From here on down, the river is very pretty, but all class 1.

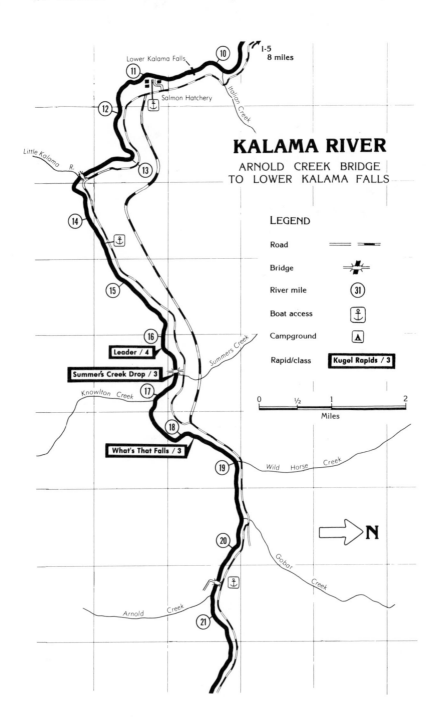

I-5
8 miles

Lower Kalama Falls

Salmon Hatchery

Italian Creek

Little Kalama R.

KALAMA RIVER
ARNOLD CREEK BRIDGE
TO LOWER KALAMA FALLS

LEGEND

Road	
Bridge	
River mile	31
Boat access	
Campground	A
Rapid/class	Kugel Rapids / 3

Summers Creek

Leader / 4

Summer's Creek Drop / 3

Knowlton Creek

What's That Falls / 3

Wild Horse Creek

0   ½   1   2
Miles

N

Gobar Creek

Arnold Creek

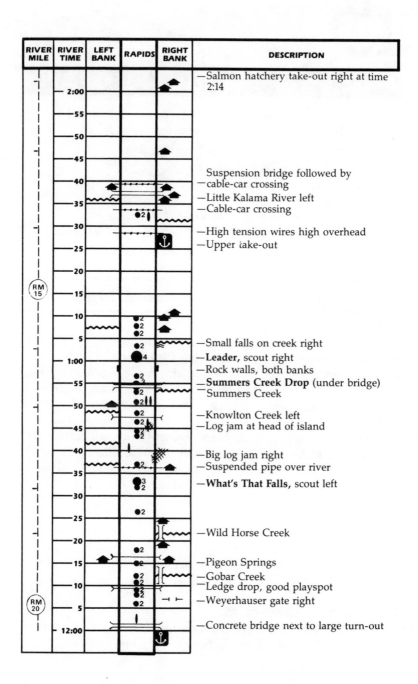

RIVER MILE	RIVER TIME	LEFT BANK	RAPIDS	RIGHT BANK	DESCRIPTION
	2:00				—Salmon hatchery take-out right at time 2:14
	45				
	40				Suspension bridge followed by —cable-car crossing
	35		●2		—Little Kalama River left —Cable-car crossing
	30				—High tension wires high overhead
	25			⚓	—Upper take-out
RM 15	10		●2 ●2 ●2		
	5		●2		—Small falls on creek right
	1:00		●4		—**Leader,** scout right —Rock walls, both banks
	55		●2 / 3 ●2		—**Summers Creek Drop** (under bridge) —Summers Creek
	50		●2 ●2 11		
	45		●2 ●2 / 2		—Knowlton Creek left —Log jam at head of island
	40				—Big log jam right
	35		●2		—Suspended pipe over river
			● 3/2		—**What's That Falls,** scout left
	30				
	25		●2		
	20				—Wild Horse Creek
	15		●2		—Pigeon Springs
	10		●2 ●2 ●2 ●2		—Gobar Creek —Ledge drop, good playspot
RM 20	5		●2		—Weyerhauser gate right
	12:00			⚓	—Concrete bridge next to large turn-out

15

Toutle

Logged at - 900 cfs Kalama gauge (March)
Recommended water level - 800 to 2,500 cfs (varies)
Best time - April through June
Rating - Expert
Water level information - NOAA Tape (206) 526-8530
NOAA Information (206) 526-6087
River mile - 16.3 to 6.8; 9.5 miles
Time - 1 hour, 58 minutes; 4.3 mph
Elevation - 420' to 115'; 32' per mile

Toutle to Tower Road Bridge

A trip on the Toutle provides a fascinating glimpse of the enormous destruction caused by the 1980 eruption of Mt. Saint Helens. Enormous mudflows roared down the Toutle valley, destroying forest, homes and bridges. Left behind are high water mud lines on the trees, many downed trees, chunks of concrete and twisted metal.

Hollywood Gorge remains an awe-inspiring solid rock cleft through which the river swirls, however; and the Toutle is rapidly cleansing itself of the enormous amount of silt and mud which choked its channel just after the eruption.

Getting There

Take exit 49 (Castle Rock) from I-5 and go 2.1 miles east on State Route 504 to Chuck's Chevron and Grocery. Just before Chuck's, Tower Road turns off of the highway to the left. Follow Tower Road 2.7 miles to the new Tower Road bridge across the Toutle.

Put-ins and Take-outs

The take-out is on the left bank on the downstream side of the bridge. To reach the put-in, either go back to Chuck's and continue 9.2 miles up State Route 504 to the new Toutle bridge (just beyond the town of Toutle), or continue across the Tower Road Bridge and follow Tower Road 10.1 miles to where it connects with State Route 504 again. If you have taken Tower Road, you should make a right and drive west on State Route 504 3.2 miles and turn left at an unmarked gravel road. Those taking State Route 504 from Chuck's will find this turn-off on their right, just 0.3 mile after crossing the Toutle bridge. The road quickly deteriorates to dirt and winds back through the trees and ends up under the Toutle bridge—the put-in.

Water Level

The Toutle has an active gauge on it at Tower Bridge, but, because of the tremendous amount of sediment carried by the Toutle, the river bed constantly changes and you cannot accurately translate the gauge height to its cfs. A reading of 12.5 feet may mean 1,000 cfs one year and 2,500 cfs the next.

Instead of using the Toutle gauge, a reasonable estimate of the flow in the Toutle can be arrived at by looking at the Kalama gauge. The Toutle should be at a good level for a first trip on the river when the Kalama is between 800 and 2,500 cfs in March, April and May, and between 500 and 1,500 cfs in June.

Boaters who know the river well may wish to run it at higher levels, but first-timers would do well to stick to these levels because it becomes very fast in both of the gorges at higher levels.

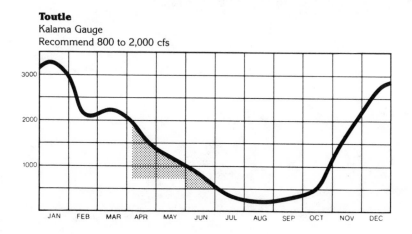

Toutle
Kalama Gauge
Recommend 800 to 2,000 cfs

Special Hazards

The Toutle demands your respect. The silt carried by the water makes it very difficult to read. The water is a uniform brown-grey, making it difficult to distinguish waves and holes. It's also important to recognize that, outside of the two gorge stretches, the river channel is still very unstable and subject to change. It changes, not just from year to year, but from day to day. You should also beware the quicksand along the river in many places. It is not difficult to pull people out with a boat, but boaters should not wander off alone along the bank where they may get stuck out of earshot of help.

The river is gradually recovering from the eruption, however; the silt decreases and the channel becomes more stable every year. In 1988 the Army Corps of Engineers will be building a dam on the river above the mouth of Green River to allow the silt to settle out. The dam should not have any effect on the water flow. While this dam will clear the water, it will prevent salmon and steelhead from reaching the upper Toutle by themselves. They will have to be trapped and trucked around the dam.

Coming out of Hollywood Gorge Falls

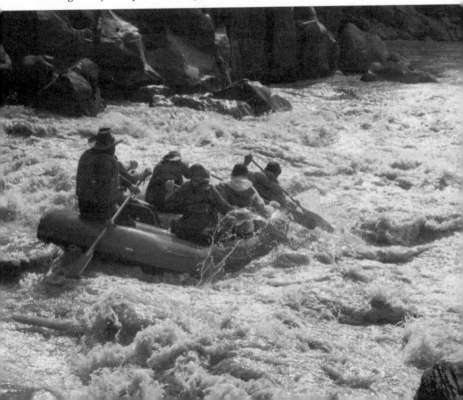

Above: The silt-laden Toutle charges through Hollywood Gorge.
Below: Debris from the flood caused by the eruption of Mount Saint Helens

Preparation of a riverside feast.

Scenery

Both gorge sections are spectacular, particularly the Hollywood Gorge from log time 1 hour, 11 minutes to 1 hour, 41 minutes. The upper gorge (from log time 3 minutes to 27 minutes) is also constricted and studded with house- and automobile-size boulders, creating interesting rapids.

The area between the gorges, from log time 38 minutes to 1 hour, 10 minutes, exhibits the enormous scouring power of the eruption. The flood plain is littered with downed trees and the land is scarred by many abandoned river channels. A particularly interesting side trip is a visit to a destroyed home, marked by the chimney, at log time 43 minutes. It's easy to land on the right bank at about log time 45 minutes and walk back to the site. The house has been buried in silt nearly eight feet deep, so that only the chimney above the mantel shows. Near the end of the devastated area, you will see mounds of material that the Army Corps of Engineers has cleared from the river channel. Bear right to stay in the main channel.

Camping

Seaquest State Park is just off State Route 504 about four miles east of Chuck's, near Silver Lake. Some additional camping is also available on a road off to the right, about three miles farther east, on the east end of Silver Lake.

Rapids

The first significant rapid of the trip is **Staircase** (or **The Steps**) at log time 11 minutes. There are huge boulders in the middle of the rapid and nasty ledges and holes to the left of them. The rapid is on a right bend in the river; stay to the right (the inside of the bend).

Tea Kettle or **Tempest in a Teapot** follows after a few hundred yards of fast water. It is around a left-hand bend and definitely deserves a scout. Land on the left bank, just below some huge boulders and above the left bend. The run threads a number of large boulders. The best route is usually just left of center in the main channel, avoiding the large hole next to the huge rocks on the right bank at the bottom.

The other rapid you should definitely scout is **Hollywood Gorge Falls** at log time 1 hour, 30 minutes. You should have no difficulty recognizing the horizon line with the huge boulder in the middle of it (covered by a mound of water at higher water levels). Land at a small beach between two rocky headlands on the right-hand side. Climb the lower headland and scramble down the rocks to get a look at the rapid. Most runs are to the left of the central rock in the falls, but at higher water levels it is also possible to spin off the rock to the right.

The major challenge of the rapid is not the falls, though you should beware the nasty lateral waves which are a lot bigger than they look from shore, but rather the hole in the center of the river about 30 yards downstream. At most water levels, this hole is preceded by a large smooth wave which saps the momentum from your boat and drops you in the hole that can easily flip an 18 foot raft. The trick is to get around the hole either to the left (very technical at high water) or the right (a tough pull in a raft).

Sand waves cause many of the class 1 rapids that create waves outside the gorges. The sand and silt carried by the river will suddenly pile up in the river bed, forming a series of waves that can just as suddenly shrink and disappear as the sand moves downriver. The Toutle river bed is constantly changing.

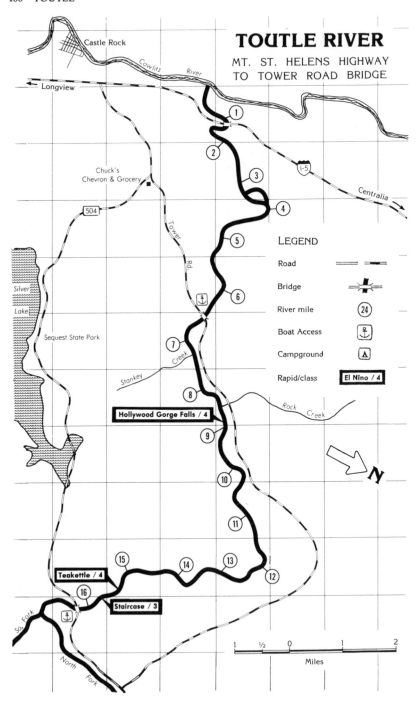

TOUTLE RIVER

MT. ST. HELENS HIGHWAY
TO TOWER ROAD BRIDGE

Castle Rock

Cowlitz River

Longview

Chuck's
Chevron & Grocery

I-5

Centralia

504

Tower Rd.

Silver Lake

Sequest State Park

Stankey

Creek

Rock Creek

LEGEND

Road	
Bridge	
River mile	24
Boat Access	⚓
Campground	⚠
Rapid/class	El Nino / 4

N

Hollywood Gorge Falls / 4

Teakettle / 4

Staircase / 3

So. Fork

North Fork

1 ½ 0 1 2
Miles

RIVER MILE	RIVER TIME	LEFT BANK	RAPIDS	RIGHT BANK	DESCRIPTION
	2:00	⚓			
	55			🏠	—Tower road bridge
	50	〰️		🏠	—Stankey Creek left
	45			🏠🏠 🏠	
	40		❙●2 ●2	🏠	
	35		●3 ●3	🏠 〰️	—Rock Creek right
	30		●4		—**Hollywood Gorge Falls,** scout right by climbing around rock headland
	25		●2 ●2 ●2		
RM 10	20		●2 ●2 ●3		
	15		●3		
	10			🏠	
	5		●2	🏠	
	1:00		●2		
	55			🏠	—Devastated Area. Remaining houses are set back from the river on bluffs
	50			🏠	
	45		❙■		—Remains of old chimney right
	40				
	35			🏠	
	30	△	●2		
				✸	—Large rock hill with trees on top right
	25	△	●2		
RM 15	20		●2 ●3		
	15	✸	●4		—**Teakettle**—run just left of center channel —Huge rocks left, land to scout **Teakettle**
	10	✸	●3 ●2		—**Staircase** (The Steps), stay right —Huge rock left
	5	■	●2 ●2		—Remains of old bridge, both banks
	12:00			⚓	—Highway bridge

16

Upper Cispus

Logged at - 2,100 cfs Randle gauge
Recommended water level - 1,500 to 2,600 cfs
Best time - April to early July
Rating - Expert
Water level information - NOAA Tape (206) 526-8530
NOAA Information (206) 526-6087
U. S. Geological Survey (206) 593-6510
River mile - 29.1 to 19.7; 9.4 miles
Time - 1 hour, 44 minutes; 5.4 mph
Elevation - 1845' to 1345'; 53' per mile

Road 23 Bridge to North Fork

The Cispus gathers its water on the west sides of Mt. Adams and the Goat Rocks and drops rapidly to the west toward its confluence with the Cowlitz. This river trip covers the portion of the Upper Cispus where its clear water tumbles through a narrow gorge in southwest Washington's Gifford Pinchot National Forest. This is one of the highest river trips possible in western Washington and snow could well block access to the river during the winter months.

The Army Corps of Engineers would like to study the feasibility of the Gravel Bar hydroelectric project which would destroy the river above Blue Lake Creek. If you would like to help save the Upper Cispus, please contact Friends of Whitewater, listed in the Preface, and get involved in the campaign to protect the Cispus as a federal Wild & Scenic River.

Getting There
The Cispus is usually approached through the town of Randle on U. S. 12. Randle is about 54 miles east of I-5 and has a Forest

Service Ranger Station. From the Puget Sound area north of Tacoma, the fastest way to Randle is on State Route 7, south through Spanaway, LaGrande and Morton to U. S. 12.

Put-ins and Take-outs

From Randle, take the Forest Service 23 road south toward Trout Lake. You'll cross the Cowlitz just after leaving Randle and, in about 1 mile, bear left toward the Cispus Environmental Center and Trout Lake. After driving about 10 miles through beautiful forest, the 28 road will turn off to the right to cross the Cispus toward the Environmental Center.

To get to the put-in, you should continue straight ahead on the 23 road toward Trout Lake. In about 10 more miles you will reach a

Heading for Smoothrock Falls

fork in the road. The pavement continues to the left toward Adams Fork Campground, but the main 23 road is the right fork. Take the right fork, which becomes a gravel road. It winds down about one mile to the river; put-in at the bridge.

There are several possible take-outs. The uppermost one is on the left bank, at about log time 1 hour, 27 minutes. To reach this take-out, take the 28 road turn-off (toward the Environmental Center) from the main 23 road and cross the bridge to the south side of the Cispus. Just 100 yards south of the river, turn left on the South Cispus road 2801. At 3.7 miles up this road you will find a spot where the river pushes against the bank just below the road (the Forest Service has protected the road by rip-rapping the bank). A good mud-flat take-out at the upper end of this bend can be reached by taking the small left channel of the river around a central boulder bar. You can get a look at **Smoothrock Falls** by driving another 1.2 miles up the 2801 road. It continues another 5 miles upriver to connect with the 23 road at the put-in.

You can also take out a little below where the North Fork joins the river. This take-out is on a broad gravel bar and requires a long carry of the equipment unless you have a four-wheel drive vehicle with high clearance which can negotiate the gravel bar. To reach this take-out, turn off the main 23 road toward the river just on the Randle side of the North Fork turn-off. A short drive will take you out on the gravel bar.

It is also possible to continue down the river to the 28 road bridge, the starting point for the lower Cispus run. Taking out here will ordinarily require one or more portages, however. The river deposits logs in this slow section of the river and all channels are usually blocked by logs in at least one place. If you attempt this section of the river, you should stay to the right where the open gravel bars offer good portage routes; don't get into the narrow, forested channels on the left. We did, on one trip and discovered the joys of pulling a raft up river through the "Okeefenokee." Hopefully, as the beauty of this trip becomes more fully appreciated, either commercial outfitters running the river or the Forest Service will take responsibility for keeping a channel open through the logs.

Water Level

The water on this portion of the river makes up about 70% of the reading on the Randle gauge. Because this trip is so steep, a change of 300 cfs can make a big difference in the power of the hydraulics. At the minimum recommended level of 1,500 cfs you will be bumping a lot of rocks and, at that level, I would not recommend the run to those with fiberglass kayaks. At the maximum recommended 2,600 cfs, you will find very powerful hydraulics and few eddies large enough for a raft. After you become familiar with the river, you may decide to run it at a higher level, but by all means, become familiar with it first because this is a very fast trip with some big drops.

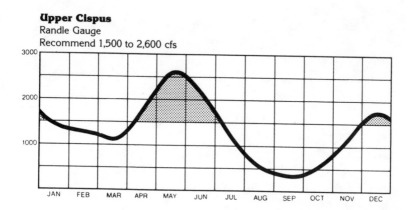

Upper Cispus
Randle Gauge
Recommend 1,500 to 2,600 cfs

Special Hazards

Logs are a special hazard on the Upper Cispus. Besides the "Okeefenokee" waiting for you below the North Fork, there is potential for log jams forming at other places on the run. Keep alert. The main channel of the river is usually blocked by logs at log time 17 minutes. It is often easy to slide your boat down the small right-hand channel, which has too little water to boat. Recently, we have encountered a log jammed between two boulders at the entrance to **Picky-Picky.** Passage around it was possible on the left, but it wouldn't hurt to scout.

Scenery

You will see almost no signs of civilization on the Upper Cispus. The road is visible in a few places, but does not often intrude through the thick forest. There are beautiful rock-walled gorges at log time 42 minutes and again at 50–55 minutes. The rock is covered with a luxuriant moss and in some places, towers

A break in a mist-shrouded descent of the Upper Cispus

25 feet over the river. The upper part of the run has a fascinating channel; it has gravel bars, small islands and chutes studded with huge boulders. In the lower part of the run, views open toward 4800′ Tongue Mountain to the west. In the early season its crags are often still frosted with snow.

You can easily understand why the Cispus is on the inventory of potential Wild & Scenic Rivers in Washington.

Camping

Numerous Forest Service campgrounds are available in the area. Adams Fork campground is about five miles above the put-in, Blue Lake Creek campground is just off the road about halfway through the run and North Fork campground is near the take-out.

Rapids

Picky-Picky, just below Juniper Creek at log time 27 minutes, provides a good warm up for the technical whitewater ahead. It doesn't require any difficult moves, but it keeps you busy with nearly a quarter mile of constant class 3 boulder dodging.

Big Bend follows a sharp left bend in the river. Pull in to the left bank to scout. It is usually run by threading through the boulders at the top to reach a pour-over ledge between a large boulder and the right bank. Then work back into the center and end the run by dropping over the bottom ledge in the center or next to the left bank. The water moves swiftly and you have to have your route well planned in advance.

White Lightning (it's white from bank to bank and you go through it like lightning) is easily recognized from upstream; you see a horizon line! A scout on the right bank will reveal a steep drop over a stair-like series of boulders. A large boulder protrudes from the water in the right-center of the channel. Most runs are made to the right of this boulder. Watch the waves at the bottom; they're bigger than they look.

Smoothrock Falls is a small falls. A solid rock ledge extends all the way across the river and the river falls some 4 to 5 feet over it. At low water you can plunge over it nearly anywhere, but at higher water levels the nearly perfect hydraulic which it creates is very dangerous. At such levels, it should be run on the right where there is a notch in the ledge which allows the water to funnel through and break the perfect hydraulic.

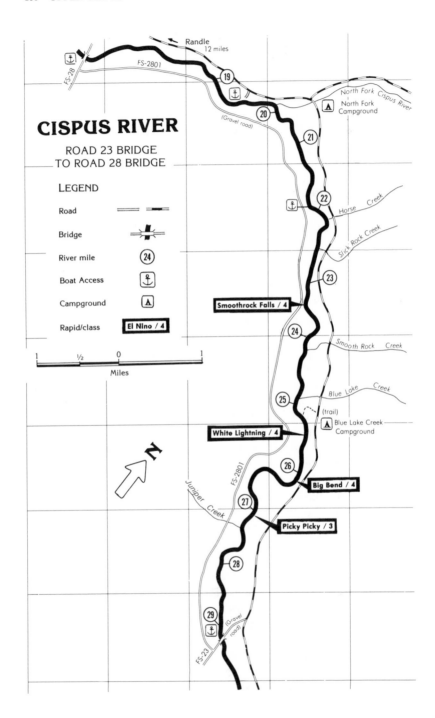

Randle
12 miles

FS-28

FS-2801

CISPUS RIVER

ROAD 23 BRIDGE
TO ROAD 28 BRIDGE

LEGEND

Road	═══ ═══
Bridge	
River mile	24
Boat Access	⚓
Campground	▲
Rapid/class	El Nino / 4

1   ½   0   1
Miles

N

(Gravel road)

19

20

21

North Fork Cispus River

North Fork
Campground

22

Horse Creek

Slick Rock Creek

23

Smoothrock Falls / 4

24

Smooth Rock Creek

25

Blue Lake Creek

(trail)

Blue Lake Creek
Campground

White Lightning / 4

26

Big Bend / 4

Juniper Creek

FS-2801

27

Picky Picky / 3

28

29

FS-23

(Gravel road)

RIVER MILE	RIVER TIME	LEFT BANK	RAPIDS	RIGHT BANK	DESCRIPTION
	2:00				
	55				
	50				—The "Okeefenokee"
	45				
RM 20	40		3		—North Fork of Cispus
	35				
	30				—Rip-rap below take-out left
	25		2		—Horse Creek
			2		—Slickrock Creek
	20		2		—Columnar basalt wall above right bank
			2		
	15		2		
			4		—Smoothrock Falls, scout left, run right
	10		2		
					—Smoothrock Creek right
	5		2		
			2		
	1:00				
			2		
RM 25	55		2		—Blue Lake Creek right
			3		—Great pop-up hole right
	50		3		
			4		—White Lightning, scout right, run right
	45		3		
			2		—Dirt cliffs right
	40		3		
			4		—Big Bend, scout left just at sharp left bend
			3		—Ledge drop, about 3 feet high
	35		3		
			3		
	30		3		—Run left side of gravel bar, crash hole
			3		—Picky Picky, Juniper Creek left
	25		2		—Rock wall to river's edge right
	20		2		
			2		Left channel blocked by logs, slide
	15		2		down right
			2		—Small waterfall left
	10		2		
			2		—Run far right of gravel bar
	5		3		
			2		—Good playspots between the
	12:00				islands

17

Skykomish, North Fork

Logged at - 7,500 cfs Goldbar gauge
Recommended water level - 6,000 to 12,000 cfs
Best time - mid-May to June
Rating - Expert
Water level information - NOAA Tape (206) 526-8530
NOAA Information (206) 526-6087
River mile - 10.7 to 0; 10.7 miles
Time - 1 hour, 59 minutes; 5.4 mph
Elevation - 1140' to 440'; 56' per mile

Galena to Confluence

Are you ready for a river that drops so fast that it disappears down through its granite boulders when you approach a major rapid? The North Fork of the Sky offers you beautiful views of the North Cascades while it puts your boating skills to the test. Hold onto your paddle, if you find the excitement is gone from the other trips in Washington guidebooks, this one will knock your socks off!

Getting There

The name Skykomish comes from the Indian words meaning "inland people." You can reach the North Fork by turning off US 2 toward the town of Index about 7.5 miles east of Goldbar. Index's 100 or so inhabitants are a mere remnant of the 1000 greed-crazed gold miners who pitched their tents in this valley in the 1890s.

Put-ins and Take-outs

About one mile up the road from US 2 toward Index, you will pass under a railroad bridge. Just before getting to the bridge,

Threading through the boulders of El Nino

there is a small dirt turn-out toward the river. This is the take-out for those running the North Fork or the put-in for those who wish to run the last mile and half of the North Fork before running the Sunset Falls stretch of the main Sky (covered in *Washington Whitewater*). Don't block this small access area by parking here. Load and unload, but park in the area off to the right (when you are coming from US 2) just *after* going under the railroad bridge. I've included the river below this point in the log for those who want to combine this trip with the main Sky.

Another put-in or take-out in this area is just across the road bridge into Index, upstream at Index City Park.

To reach the put-in continue up the North Fork road nearly 10 miles to where the road crosses the river on a new concrete bridge. About 150 yards beyond the bridge is a large turn-out next to the river: the put-in. The eddies amongst the rocks here are small and a raft has to be tied up because at least part of it is going to be out in the current.

Alternative put-ins for those who would like to reduce the amount of white-knuckle whitewater but still see most of the scenery are just above Trout Creek and just below the bridge near Howard Creek (on the left bank) at log time 18 minutes. This bridge is reached by turning off toward the river about one mile short of the bridge near the upper put-in, or about nine miles above the take-out.

Water Level

The North Fork provides 39% of the water recorded on the Goldbar gauge. Because of the enormous number of boulders studding its course, a lot of water is needed to boat the river. Kayakers can boat the river at 4,000 cfs and rafts can run the river from the bridge above Howard Creek on 5,000 cfs, but 6,000 cfs is necessary to raft the upper part of the river.

Boaters familiar with the North Fork will run it at higher levels than recommended here, but there is little margin for error at higher flows. At the logged level of 7,500 cfs there were few eddies large enough for a raft and landing was difficult in the upper part of the run.

Special Hazards

Find out about logs on the river before you go; the logs change position every year. There are often logs which you must avoid, particularly in the section a little below the bridge at log time 18 minutes, where the river has recently cut a new channel for itself through the forest. In 1986, a flood deposited a log in this area which completely blocked the river channel. The best way to find out about log conditions is to contact the Washington Kayak Club (WKC), whose members regularly run the North Fork of the Sky. Join the WKC and stay on top of boating conditions in Washington: Box 24264, Seattle, WA 98124. If you can't find anyone who has run the river recently, walk along the bank to check for log jams *before* you start down the river in your boat.

Skykomish, North Fork
Goldbar Gauge
Recommend 6,000 to 12,000 cfs

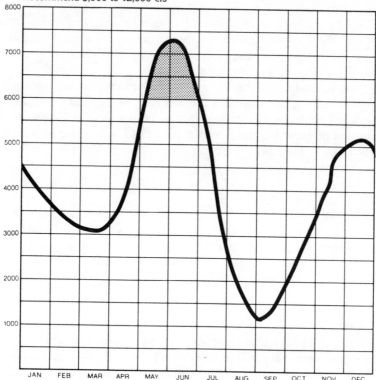

Scenery

Although there are numerous cabins near Index and at two other points farther upriver, the river banks are largely natural. Huge granite boulders punctuating the narrow upper river channel make the first mile of the trip very interesting, if you can find a moment to think of anything besides the rapids. Gorgeous views of snow-capped Gunn Peak to the east and Mt. Index and Mt. Persis to the south open up as you descend to the middle of the run and the whitewater lets up enough to allow you to look around occasionally. As you approach the end of the trip, you will have good views of the Index Town Wall, behind the town of Index to the northwest, and may see a few of the many rock climbers who train there.

The North Fork of the Skykomish is a wintering area for bald eagles. They are particularly active in feeding during December and January, so it is best to avoid boating the river during those months when you might disturb them.

Unfortunately, the beauty of the North Fork is endangered. Boaters and conservationists are working on legislation to have the North Fork designated as a Federal Wild & Scenic River to stop the dam planned for the river upstream of the boating section. If you'd like to help save the North Fork, contact Friends of Whitewater, listed in the Preface.

Camping

Troublesome Creek is about 1.0 mile and San Juan Forest Service Campgrounds are about 3.0 miles up the North Fork valley above the put-in. These campgrounds are usually open only between Memorial Day and Labor Day.

Rapids

Ah, the rapids. These are long, rocky haircurlers which challenge you with 200 yards of continuous class 3+ and then end in a substantial class 4 drop. After running the first two miles of the North Fork for the first time, I was shell-shocked. Around river mile 10 the river slope is about 120 feet per mile, nearly the steepest that can be rafted. The clear waters of the North Fork offer some of the best whitewater in Washington. County ordinance requires everyone to wear helmets and life jackets on both the North Fork and main Skykomish above Goldbar.

The first big drop, **El Nino** (Guardrail), is right next to the road and should be obvious on the shuttle since the road is generally screened from the river by trees, but not here. Take a look at **El Nino** on the shuttle, you won't have much time to look at it when you're on the river. The other stand-out piece of whitewater is the **Minefield**, full of unexpected holes. You may want to scout it on the left, it's trickier than it looks from the river. The North Fork offers the most continually challenging run covered by Washington guidebooks.

Boulders nearly choke the North Fork's channel.

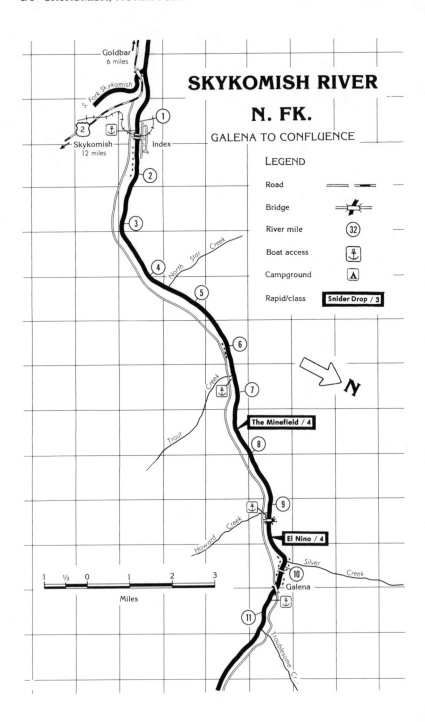

Goldbar
6 miles

S. Fork Skykomish

Skykomish
12 miles

Index

SKYKOMISH RIVER
N. FK.
GALENA TO CONFLUENCE

LEGEND

Road	
Bridge	
River mile	32
Boat access	⚓
Campground	⛺
Rapid/class	**Snider Drop / 3**

North Star Creek

N

Creek

Trout

The Minefield / 4

Howard Creek

El Nino / 4

Silver Creek

Galena

Troublesome Cr.

1 ½ 0 1 2 3

Miles

RIVER MILE	RIVER TIME	LEFT BANK	RAPIDS	RIGHT BANK	DESCRIPTION
RM 0	2:00				—South Fork Skykomish left
	55				—Powerlines
					—Take left channel around big island with trees
	50				—Powerlines
					—Difficult class 3, enter far left, move right
	45				
	40				—Index Bridge
	35				
	30				
	25				
	20				—Keep to left side of right channel
	15				—Hazardous rock wall to right of gravel bar
	10				—North Star Creek right
					—Beautiful eddy and large beach left
RM 5	5				
	1:00				
	55				—Cable crossing, run either side of gravel bar
	50				—Trout Creek left
					—Rock with concrete square on it right
	45				
	40				—The Minefield, scout left, start left, work center
	35				—Cable crossing
	30				—Fun waves
	25				—Large island with trees left
	20				—Howard Creek left
	15				—El Nino, scout from road, run left
					—Silver Creek right
RM 10	10				—Galena Bridge
	5				
	12:00				

Appendix

In 1986, the Washington State Legislature passed a law governing commercial river running. While the provisions apply only to commercial trips, all river runners should comply with some of the sections. **Section 3** requires that all watercraft be operated in a careful and prudent manner and that no watercraft interfere with other watercraft or proper navigation of the river. **Section 9** spells out the reporting requirements in the event that a person dies or disappears.

Passenger-Carrying Watercraft— Regulation
Chapter 217, Senate Bill No. 4990

AN ACT Relating to river running; adding a new chapter to Title 91 RCW; and prescribing penalties.

BE IT ENACTED BY THE LEGISLATURE OF THE STATE OF WASHINGTON:

NEW SECTION. Sec. 1. The purpose of this chapter is to further the public interest, welfare, and safety by providing for the protection and promotion of safety in the operation of watercraft carrying passengers for hire on the rivers of this state.

NEW SECTION. Sec. 2. Unless the context clearly requires otherwise, the definitions in this section apply throughout this chapter.
(1) "Watercraft" means every type of watercraft carrying passengers for hire used as a means of transportation on a river, including but not limited to power boats, drift boats, open canoes, inflatable crafts, decked canoes, and kayaks.
(2) "Carrying passengers for hire" means carrying passengers by watercraft for valuable consideration, whether given directly or indirectly or received by the owner, agent, operator, or other person having an interest in the watercraft. This shall not affect trips where expenses for food, transportation, or incidentals are shared by participants on an even basis. Anyone receiving compensation for skills or money for amortization of equipment and carrying passengers shall be considered to be carrying passengers for hire. Individuals licensed under chapter 77.32 RCW and acting as a fishing guide are exempt from this chapter.
(3) "Operate" means to navigate or otherwise use a watercraft.
(4) "Operator" means any person operating the watercraft or performing

the duties of a pilot or guide for one or more watercraft in a group.

(5) "Passenger" means every person on board a watercraft who is not an operator.

(6) "Rivers of the state" means those rivers and streams, or parts thereof, within the boundaries of this state.

NEW SECTION. Sec. 3. (1) No person may operate any watercraft in a manner that interferes with other watercraft or with the free and proper navigation of the rivers of this state.

(2) Every operator of a watercraft shall at all times operate the watercraft in a careful and prudent manner and at such a speed as to not endanger the life, limb, or property of any person.

(3) No watercraft may be loaded with passengers or cargo beyond its safe carrying capacity taking into consideration the type and construction of the watercraft and other existing operating conditions. In the case of inflatable crafts, safe carrying capacity in whitewater shall be considered as less than the United States Coast Guard capacity rating for each watercraft. This subsection shall not apply in cases of an unexpected emergency on the river.

NEW SECTION. Sec. 4. (1) Except as provided in subsection (2) of this section, watercraft proceeding downstream have the right of way over watercraft proceeding upstream.

(2) In all cases, watercraft not under power have the right of way over motorized craft underway.

NEW SECTION. Sec. 5. (1) No person may operate on the rivers of this state a watercraft carrying passengers for hire unless the person has been issued a valid Red Cross standard first aid card or at least its equivalent.

(2) This section does not apply to a person operating a vessel on the navigable waters of the United States in this state and who is licensed by the United States Coast Guard for the type of vessel being operated.

NEW SECTION. Sec. 6. While carrying passengers for hire on whitewater river sections in this state, the operator and owner shall:

(1) If using inflatable watercraft, use only watercraft with three or more separate air chambers;

(2) Ensure that all passengers and operators are wearing a securely fastened United States Coast Guard approved type III or type V life jacket in good condition;

(3) Ensure that each watercraft has accessible a spare type III or type V life jacket in good repair;

(4) Ensure that each watercraft has on it a bagged throwable line with a floating line and bag;

(5) Ensure that each watercraft has accessible an adequate first-aid kit;

(6) Ensure that each watercraft has a spare propelling device;

(7) Ensure that a repair kit and air pump are accessible to inflatable watercraft; and

(8) Ensure that equipment to prevent and treat hypothermia is accessible to all watercraft on a trip.

NEW SECTION. Sec. 7. (1) Watercraft operators and passengers on any trip carrying passengers for hire shall not allow the use of alcohol during the course of a trip on a whitewater river section in this state.

(2) Any watercraft carrying passengers for hire on any whitewater river section in this state must be accompanied by at least one other watercraft under the supervision of the same operator or owner or being operated by a person registered under section 11 of this act or an operator under the direction or control of a person registered under section 11 of this act.

NEW SECTION. Sec. 8. Whitewater river sections include but are not limited to:

(1) Green river above Flaming Geyser state park;

(2) Klickitat river above the confluence with Summit creek;

(3) Methow river below the town of Carlton;

(4) Sauk river above the town of Darrington;

(5) Skagit river above Bacon creek;

(6) Suiattle river;

(7) Tieton river below Rimrock dam;

(8) Skykomish river below Sunset Falls and above the Highway 2 bridge one mile east of the town of Gold Bar;

(9) Wenatchee river above the Wenatchee county park at the town of Monitor;

(10) White Salmon river; and

(11) Any other section of river designated a "whitewater river section" by the interagency committee for outdoor recreation. Such river sections shall be class two or greater difficulty under the international scale of whitewater difficulty.

NEW SECTION. Sec. 9. (1) When, as a result of an occurrence that involves a watercraft or its equipment, a person dies or disappears from a watercraft, the operator shall notify the nearest sheriff's department, state patrol office, coast guard station, or other law enforcement agency of:

(a) The date, time, and exact location of the occurrence;

(b) The name of each person who died or disappeared;

(c) A description of the watercraft; and

(d) The names and addresses of the owner and operator.

(2) When the operator of a boat cannot give the notice required by subsection (1) of this section, each person on board the boat shall either give the notice or determine that the notice has been given.

NEW SECTION. Sec. 10. (1) Every peace officer of this state and its political subdivisions has the authority to enforce this chapter. Wildlife agents of the department of game and fisheries patrol officers of the department of fisheries, through their directors, the state patrol, through its chief, county sheriffs, and other local law enforcement bodies, shall assist in the enforcement. In the exercise of this responsibility, all such officers may stop any watercraft and direct it to a suitable pier or anchorage for boarding.

(2) A person, while operating a watercraft on any waters of this state, shall not knowingly flee or attempt to elude a law enforcement officer after having received a signal from the law enforcement officer to bring the boat to a stop.

(3) This chapter shall be construed to supplement federal laws and regulations. To the extent this chapter is inconsistent with federal laws and regulations, the federal laws and regulations shall control.

NEW SECTION. Sec. 11. (1) Any person carrying passengers for hire on whitewater river sections in this state may register with the department of licensing. Each registration application shall be submitted annually on a form provided by the department of licensing and shall include the following information:

(a) The name, residence address, and residence telephone number, and the business name, address, and telephone number of the registrant;

(b) Proof that the registrant has liability insurance for a minimum of three hundred thousand dollars per claim for occurrences by the registrant and the registrant's employees that result in bodily injury or property damage; and

(c) Certification that the registrant will maintain the insurance for a period of not less than one year from the date of registration.

(2) The department of licensing shall charge a fee for each application, to be set in accordance with RCW 43.24.086.

(3) Any person advertising or representing themselves as having registered under this section who is not currently registered is guilty of a gross misdemeanor.

(4) The department of licensing shall submit annually a list of registered persons and companies to the department of trade and economic development, tourism promotion division.

(5) If an insurance company cancels or refuses to renew insurance for a registrant during the period of registration, the insurance company shall notify the department of licensing in writing of the termination of coverage and its effective date not less than thirty days before the effective date of termination.

(a) Upon receipt of an insurance company termination notice, the department of licensing shall send written notice to the registrant that on the effective date of termination the department of licensing will suspend the registration unless proof of insurance as required by this section is filed with the department of licensing before the effective date of the termination.

(b) If an insurance company fails to give notice of coverage termination, this failure shall not have the effect of continuing the coverage.

(c) The department of licensing may suspend or revoke registration under this section if the registrant fails to maintain in full force and effect the insurance required by section 11 of this act.

(6) The state of Washington shall be immune from any civil action arising from a registration under this section.

NEW SECTION. Sec. 12. A person violating this chapter shall be subject to a civil penalty of up to one hundred fifty dollars per violation.

NEW SECTION. Sec. 13. Sections 1 through 12 of this act shall constitute a new chapter in Title 91 RCW.

Approved April 2, 1986.
Effective June 11, 1986, 90 days after date of adjournment.

Index

*The author taping
notes on a whitewater trip.*

Doug North began running Washington rivers six years ago as a whitewater canoeist. He was surprised to find out that little information on Washington's whitewater rivers was available in print; particularly lacking was information on good water levels for each trip. So he began compiling information that resulted in his guidebooks — first, *Washington Whitewater* and now, *Washington Whitewater 2*.

North is a Washington native and practices law in Seattle. A long-time outdoor enthusiast, he also hikes, climbs and skis cross-country. In addition to boating Washington rivers, he has run nearly a dozen rivers in Colorado, Oregon, Idaho and British Columbia. A founder of Friends of Whitewater, he has been very active in protecting the rivers of the Northwest from development that would interfere with their free-flowing qualities and the recreation, fish and wildlife dependent on them.